CW00504408

THE WOMAN WHO NEVER WAS

by

Jane Doe as told to Cyril Clements

JANE DOE 1923 PUBLISHING COMPANY

THE WOMAN WHO NEVER WAS

ISBN 978-0-9571331-0-5

First published in Great Britain by
Jane Doe 1923 Publishing Company
5 Hardstoft Road
Pilsley
Chesterfield
S45 8BL
www.janedoe.co.uk

Printed in Great Britain by
www.direct-pod.com

THE WOMAN WHO NEVER WAS

To NORMA

Jack Dale

Author's note

This real life account of Jane Doe is indeed a truly amazing story which tells of one woman's unending struggle to establish her true identity. Jane's earliest memories go back to when she was a normal, happy little girl called Barbara, living with a loving couple whom she thought of as her mummy and daddy, in a picturesque Hertfordshire village. She remembers the village school and the pond across the green, where she would be taken to feed the ducks. She remembers the toys she played with for hours – some of them lovingly made for her by 'Daddy', and she has fond memories of her little bedroom with its warm, cosy feather bed.

One memory will never fade: the warm spring day more than eighty years ago now, when some itinerant travellers knocked on the door of the cottage and said they had come to claim their child. One minute she was happily playing with her dolls, the next she found herself being bundled into the horse-drawn 'Varda' wagon by a dark-haired, dark-eyed, rough looking man who smelt of wood smoke. He said he was Robert Hall, and the woman was Violet, his wife. There was another child in the 'Varda' – Lily, Barbara's half-sister, who kicked her spitefully in a jealous rage,saying "They're my parents, not yours!"

As the story unfolds, Jane reveals how she was verbally, physically, mentally and sexually abused by her so-called parents as she was forced to travel the countryside with them. Violet was often drunk and, had a vicious temper and would shout and swear at both girls, at times beating them mercilessly. Robert was not unkind to young Barbara, but would await his opportunity and then take her to his bed, warning her that she would be taken away and put in a home if she told anyone.

2

Barbara grew up and started work. At eighteen, she went to work at Luxfers, a munitions factory, where she earned the respect of her employers and work colleagues, and was soon entrusted with the responsibility of driving the dillies carrying loaded bombs. The family had by then ceased to travel the highways and now lived in a house nearby. She was frequently locked out and forced to sleep in the outside toilet – presumably a punishment from Violet for daring to have a social life. One night while she was out with her workmates, she met George, a young sailor home on leave from his ship. They began a relationship and Barbara was over the moon when he asked her to marry him and readily accepted his proposal – she would at last be free of the insults and constant rowing. The sexual abuse and beatings may have stopped, but her life was far from what it should be for a young person now in her twenties. But what Barbara didn't know then was that the freedom and normality she so craved would turn to ashes; her past was to haunt her for the rest of her life.

The signs were there before the wedding, but Barbara had no understanding then of the legalities; frankly, she didn't care a hoot as long as she could escape from the clutches of this family and begin to live a normal life… and who could blame her? The registrar said she would have to come back with her birth certificate… and bring her father. There was an unholy row when she told them at home. Violet became hysterical, but Robert calmly put his coat on and went with Barbara to 'sort this out'. Barbara was made to sit outside in the corridor whilst Robert spoke to the registrar. She had no idea what was said and has never known to this day; but there was a thinly veiled threat from the Registrar who menacingly wagged his finger and told her that she could go ahead and marry, but if she ever discussed this meeting with anyone, both she and her father would get six months in jail.

3

Even the wedding day itself was fraught with delays because the correct procedures had not been followed and hasty phone calls had to be made before the marriage could go ahead. But before the day was over, Barbara Hall became Barbara Worrall.

More than twenty years (and six children) later, Barbara became uneasy about her status in life – her mind kept going back to her childhood days, and the mysteries that she had never been able to solve. Remembering the fuss about her birth certificate, she decided to go back to the same registry office and obtain a copy for herself. At the first attempt she was told there was no birth certificate for anyone called Barbara Hall. No explanation was given and she was sent away after being made to feel a nuisance. She returned at a later date and, insisting upon her rights, was eventually handed the document that, she was told, was her birth certificate. Her elation quickly turned to despair and desolation when she read its contents: Father's name Robert Mark Shaw; mother's name Violet Shaw, formerly Goss… but she was Barbara Hall, wasn't she? When she queried it, insisting there had been a mistake, she was told, '…no mistake – that is your birth certificate.'

So who was she? Her past now became a dark shadow that followed wherever she went; she questioned the validity of her marriage and, after much soul-searching, she made the decision to leave her family – too ashamed to be called Mother by six illegitimate children, for that was surely what they were, she told herself. Her marriage was a sham, an untruth, just like her birth certificate, and she could no longer carry on living the lie.

Around that time, whilst playing bingo, she bumped into a childhood friend, Cyril Clements. She had been a friend of Cyril's older sister and even remembered helping to bath him when he was a young boy. They instantly recognised each other and had a drink together, talking over old times. Their meetings became more frequent and within a short time, the couple had fallen in love. Barbara left a note for her family and set off to find Clem's flat. When he arrived home from work that evening, she had a meal ready for him and told him she'd like to stay and look after him, if he'd let her.

True love stands the test of time and, the couple have not been parted since that day in 1967. However, Clem knew nothing of Barbara's problems and only realized that something was terribly wrong in her life when she began having bad dreams and shouting in her sleep, "Who am I?" When Barbara eventually managed to tell the full story to Clem, he was horrified, naturally, and vowed that he would do whatever it took to solve the mystery of her birth and indeed, he has steadfastly devoted his life to her cause. Clem, says Jane, is her rock. Sadly, in spite of Clem's gargantuan efforts, the mystery remains unsolved.

Jane's heartbreaking story is told within these pages – no punches pulled. From Barbara, the lonely ill-treated little girl, right up to the present strong and, determined woman who is Jane Doe. A dignified octogenarian now, she reveals the truth about her childhood and the frequent visits by Henry Hall, the famous bandleader, when he would bring her lavish presents, sit her on his knee and call her 'Lady Barbara'; how she and Clem went on a mission to find Roxley Cottages, from where she was abducted that sunny, spring morning; two bigamous marriages to Clem, and the child she bore him – a miracle, as she had been sterilised – and the problems encountered when registering his birth. The relentless search for any clue that might help to establish who her natural parents really were... has there been a conspiracy, a cover-up? And if so why? At every turn, Jane has been denied the truth about the one thing she desperately wanted to know. She is Jane Doe now – a piece of paper says so, a change of name deed, and it's legal.

But who is she really? Why was her birth certificate falsified? And by whom? Will she ever find the answers… who knows? But until she does, Jane Doe will remain the woman who never was, along with all the other Jane Does in the world, for whom this book has been written.

Birth details

Born to parents Robert Mark Shaw and Violet Shaw, formerly Violet Goss. Birth delivery by forceps – doctor is believed to be present. Request to attend by midwife. Weight at time of birth 10lbs 8ozs. Inception of birth June 9, 1923, registration district Nottingham. Birth in the sub-district of Nottingham North East pursuant to the Births and Deaths Registration Act and recorded at the Register Office, Shakespeare Street, Nottingham. Superintendent Registrar for the District of Nottingham in the County Borough of Nottingham C.H. Truman, search made by the Mormon Genealogical Records Computer Centre, Salt Lake City, Utah, USA can find no marriage of the aforementioned, but have supplied evidence of a marriage in the Registration District Nottingham, marriage solemnised at the Register Office, District of Nottingham in the County of Nottingham pursuant to the marriage Act on 18th July 1919, Sydney Shaw 20 years bachelor, Carter, 9 Foundry Yard Leen Side Nottingham. Charles Shaw father deceased farm labourer, Violet Goss 18 years spinster, 14 Ivy Row Brook Street, Nottingham. William Goss father, Slater, Registrar H. Clarke, Superintendent Registrar, J. Allan Battersby witnessed in the presence J. Woodford, Arnie Woodford.

No evidence of the existence of Robert Mark Shaw has ever been located. Enquiry has been hampered to the whereabouts of these persons due to the microfiche for the electoral roll having gone missing from Nottingham Records.

BARBARA SHAW
Date and Place of Birth   May 20, 1923
30 Cross Street, City of Nottingham, England
Date and Place of Death   Unknown
Missing since birth   Presumed dead
Office years 1915/1931

7

Revelation

Before my days on earth are through
I would be a person just like you
I would like to know, before I die
Why was my life a created lie?
The story is, a Name, protected
From himself, sin undetected
No matter that a child is left
As human wreckage, now bereft.
Amongst the Good and Great is born
A Plan, to leave this child forlorn
To take away Identity
To change an infant's destiny
The Great and Good were not to know
That times would soon be changing so.
To tug the forelock and bend the knee
We're not so ready now, you see.
The Time is now, the Day is come
A Story that is now begun
May bring relief and end my pain
By granting me one wish -
MY NAME

Prologue

Proof of identity is a basic human right which most of us take for granted. We know who we are; who our forebears were and we have documents to support and verify our existence. However, this right has been denied Jane Doe for eighty-three years. She knows that the birth certificate issued to her by a Nottingham registrar in 1967 is a fabrication.

The repercussions of this falsehood led eventually to Jane leaving her husband and six children. Her false birth certificate obviously meant that her marriage in 1945 was not legal and all her children were therefore illegitimate. Such was her shame and abhorrence of having lived such a lie for twenty-two years that she walked out on them in 1967, never to return. Jane had been a good wife and mother and loved each of her children dearly and we can hardly begin to imagine the mental anguish she must have suffered to take such a drastic step.

What became of Jane following her dramatic and uncharacteristic action begins to unfold in Chapter One of her harrowing yet compelling story. The reader will learn of the complex events leading to her heart-rending decision; how a normal, happy childhood was snatched away from her by strangers and, in later life, other fundamental social rights, including lawful marriage and re-marriage, holidays abroad and a retirement pension in her own right, have been denied her through no fault of her own. Jane has no legal identity; therefore she has no nationality and no passport. Furthermore, her 'pension' is based on somebody else's National Insurance number. Jane herself is blameless and therefore without any control over the circumstances in which she finds herself, which makes it all the more distressing.

There are many others in a similar predicament to Jane, for whatever reasons, but few can have experienced worse treatment by the so-called authorities – those who, instead of being helpful and sympathetic to Jane's plight, have mercilessly swept their own dirt under the carpet and then washed their hands of her. These individuals do not observe and perpetuate the law - they aspire, maybe even conspire, to be above the law. A handful of well-intentioned professionals have found themselves retreating smartly before the might of the bureaucratic wall. Their hard hats of morality and fair play afford little protection from the force of the iniquitous power produced by closed ranks.

As Jane's story continues, the closed ranks become locked and bolted. Who, or what, is able to shatter the impenetrable? Within these pages ticks a time-bomb, which can only be detonated by the truth - buried at the centre of Jane's life since birth.

Jane is eighty-three now. She has endured a lifetime of crippling uncertainty which continues to torment her to this day and will do so until she reaches her goal in life which so far has proved to be so elusive. That goal, before she dies, is to discover exactly who she is and by making the courageous decision to publish this heart-rending account of her experiences, Jane is sincere in her wish to give hope and moral support to others out there who find themselves in similar circumstances.

Chapter 1   Dear Family

I suppose it was quite a shock for you all, the day I walked out on you, never to return ~ and there are those of you who have never forgiven me. At the time, I was in a state of shock. Shock at the way I had been deceived by the couple you came to know as your grandparents. How was I to explain my feelings when I learned of my birth certificate? I wasn't clever but I knew enough to tell me that my birth certificate name should have been on your birth certificates and then I realized that I was living a lie. Was it wrong of me to be concerned about you all ~ to feel that it was my duty, no matter what, to seek out the truth, or you might inherit the legacy of lies that I was now fully aware of?

When I left you, it was just something that happened and when it did, I knew there was no turning back. Events dictated my life from the moment I knew about my birth. My book, when it is published, will reveal all and I have no doubts about its publication. One day you will know who your real grandparents were.

The book reveals (or tells about) your true grandmother. As for your grandfather, for his identity you will have to wait until possibly you are the same age as I am now. I would not wish for you to endure the persecution, apprehension and torment that have been ours for these past twenty-five years.

I have no regrets about my past. What happened, happened? I cannot turn the clock back. I consider that I was a good wife and mother and I am proud of the way I brought you up in difficult times.

Clem has been very good to me. He has put up a very courageous fight against all the odds. I now intend to start to enjoy retirement and owe all of this to Clem. One day we will marry legally.

The previous letter is not the one I wrote when I walked out on my husband and six children in 1967. That was just a scribbled note to inform them that I was leaving. This letter is something I have felt compelled to write and which has come from my heart. I have been criticized for being a bad wife and uncaring mother and have been told that no mother who loved her children would even think of deserting them in any circumstances. My critics know nothing of my situation and they are wrong in saying that I was bad, uncaring or unloving. It was precisely because I loved them – all of them, that I did what I did on that sunny autumn day all those years ago.

When I married George Worrall in 1945 in the name of Barbara Hall, the birth certificate used to identify me and confirm my age had been falsified. I already knew that something was wrong. The difficulties I had encountered with the registrars in Nottingham and Bristol had taught me that much. At the time of my marriage, however, birth records were not the most important issue in my life. I was twenty-two years old, had found a man whom I thought was genuinely going to love and care for me and take me away at last from the living hell that had been my home life for seventeen years.

I did wonder why there was such secrecy surrounding my birth and why there had been such hoo-ha at home when I told Robert and Violet that I needed my birth certificate. Also, there was the thinly veiled threat from the registrar that if I didn't keep my mouth shut I would be responsible for both him and Robert being locked up for six months. However, all of these things were of little concern to me at that time.

It was much later on, as my responsibilities grew in proportion to the size the family had then reached, that I began to have flashbacks of my childhood and early teens and the issues regarding my birth certificate at the time of our marriage began to surface and disturb my peace of mind. It was rather like an itch that I couldn't reach, but which eventually became so troublesome it just had to be scratched. Once you start scratching it can be hard to stop, and I found myself heading for the

Registry Office in Shakespeare Street, Nottingham. I wanted to obtain a copy of my birth certificate so that I could reassure myself that everything was in order. I longed for the confidence to be myself but in reality felt very unsure about who I really was.

Imagine how shocked I felt when the registrar informed me that there were no birth records for Barbara Hall. I stared at him open-mouthed. "But there must be a mistake," I protested. "I was born on 20th May, 1923 at..."

His reply cut me off sharply.

"I assure you, Madam," emphasizing the Madam in a rather sarcastic manner, "That there is no mistake. I repeat, there is no birth certificate for a Barbara Hall."

He told me that I would have to obtain more information about the date and place of my birth, which would enable him to carry out a further search of the records. He then dismissively turned his back to me, reinforcing my rapidly growing feeling that I really was non-existent.

Puzzled, bewildered and humiliated, I left the premises. Where or to whom could I turn now? I had not confided my fears to another living soul and still didn't feel able to discuss it. I felt miserably isolated. I had once tried to broach the subject with George, but he was simply not interested in any of it and refused to listen.

I did nothing for a while but then the uncertainty and suspicion began to fester inside me. The situation was becoming intolerable and affecting my everyday life. I decided that I would try once more and, screwing up every available ounce of courage, I returned to Shakespeare Street, promising myself that I would not leave without my birth certificate.

This time, I received a slightly more civil reception, but I still found the supercilious attitude of the registrar very unnerving. I had brought my marriage certificate with me and presented it to him. At least that proved I was a person…didn't it? After what seemed like an eternity, he came back with a folded document in his hand.

"Here you are Mrs. Worrall. Your birth certificate."

Elated, I thanked him, almost snatching the paper from his hand, and rushed outside with it. Now perhaps I could settle down and get on with the rest of my life. My fears could be laid to rest.

Imagine then the bitter disappointment that overwhelmed me when, safely out of view round the corner, I unfolded the document only to discover that it recorded the birth, not of Barbara Hall, but Barbara Shaw. I could hardly believe my eyes. In a tearful state and with my heart in my boots, I went back inside the registry office to confront the registrar.

"This is not my birth certificate," I protested, holding the offending document out to him. "My name was never Shaw, it has always been Hall!"

Unmoved, the registrar simply confirmed that it was the only one relating to the child born on 20th May 1923 at Cross Street. When I began to argue with him he turned on me, suggesting menacingly that it would be for my own good if I were to take the document and leave the premises immediately.

So emotionally and mentally confused was I that the next few days just passed in a daze of disbelief. The unthinkable had happened. I had for some time harboured strange feelings that there had been something very odd and mysterious about my birth and now I had the unmistakable evidence that I really was not who I thought I was. Slowly, the implications for my family dawned on me. I had married as Barbara Hall. My birth certificate said I was Barbara Shaw. Was I legally married? Most probably not. The idea that I had brought six illegitimate children into the world was too much to bear. I felt that I was unworthy of them, that they did not deserve any of this. Neither did I, for that matter. I was not to blame for any of it, but certainly I was going to be the one to feel the shame and carry the stigma.

These negative thoughts and feelings continued to grow like a gnawing cancer inside me. I had no-one to confide in and often felt that I was going quietly insane. It was a very lonely time. Then another door opened unexpectedly in my life when I met up again with an old friend, Cyril 'Clem' Clements. That chance meeting changed my life and gave me fresh hope for the future. I fell in love with him and left my home and family to be with him. But it was many months later before I was able to even begin to tell him my story, when he finally insisted that I give him an explanation for my frequent and unsettling nightmares.

Chapter 2   Whit Sunday

The leading news story on 20th May 1923, Whit Sunday, was the shock resignation of Prime Minister Andrew Bonar-Law who, having been in office for only six months, was reportedly bowing out due to ill health. Indeed, it transpired later that Bonar-Law had been diagnosed with the terminal throat cancer that claimed his life in October 1923 – just a year after first entering 10 Downing Street. Mr. Bonar-Law is quoted as once saying, "If I am a great man, then a good many great men of history are frauds." This head of government was apparently a modest and unassuming man with hidden depths. No doubt these qualities gave rise to his nickname, which was 'The Unknown Prime Minister'. There are two key words here that I can apply to my own life.

Fraud is a word I can identify with. It is defined in the Oxford dictionary as criminal deception; the use of false representations to gain an unjust advantage; a dishonest artifice or trick, and lastly, a person or thing not fulfilling what is claimed or expected of it. Unknown is another word that I can readily apply to my own circumstances.

The Whitsuntide weather was nondescript. Overcast, not really that warm, nor too cold. Maybe a little disappointing for those planning a Bank Holiday outing, but unremarkable. Unlike the events taking place in a small back bedroom of the dwelling known as 30 Cross Street in the City of Nottingham, where a baby girl was making her entrance into the world. She was a bonny, bouncing baby, too, weighing in at 10lbs 8oz, and her delivery had to be assisted by the use of forceps.

Midwives were not then qualified to use forceps, so a doctor must have attended this particular birth. However, no doctor is recorded as being present and a note from the Principal Archivist of Nottinghamshire County Council states that "The midwives' records for the 1920s have been closed to public inspection because they contain personal and possibly sensitive information on possible illegitimacies, etc."

When details of this birth were registered nearly three weeks later, on 9th June, the little girl was named as Barbara Shaw. Her father was entered as Robert Mark Shaw, a farm labourer, and her mother was Violet Shaw, formerly Violet Goss. However, no record of that particular Robert Mark Shaw has ever been traced – he did not exist. What is incredible is the fact that there was no trace of this child for the next forty years. Officially, Barbara Shaw did not exist either.

Cross Street was but a few paces away from the Central Market, Sneinton Market, the Victoria Ballroom and the Palais de Danse, all very popular venues at that time, particularly at weekends and holiday times. A handful of back streets and alleyways further on was the infamous Narrow Marsh area where Violet, in company with her glamorous sister Lily (a prostitute) and brother Billy with his glass eye, would frequent notorious pubs such as the Red Lion, The Loggerheads (still open today), and the Old Volunteer, to name but a few. Other favourites with this merry trio were the Corner Pin, and the Old Dog & Partridge in Parliament Street.

Violet's main talent lay in the art of bending the elbow and being generally ill natured. Lily, on the other hand, was very friendly. She was no mean whistler and, with Billy yodelling in accompaniment, entertained the punters whilst no doubt weighing up one or two possible clients for later.

Old Narrow Marsh was known as the worst slum area of the city, with as many as five hundred people to an acre, mostly living in overcrowded and filthy tenements. Murder, rape, and prostitution were all commonplace in the squalid streets and it is interesting to note that many of the criminal acts, including murder, were perpetrated by women. Narrow Marsh women of the day were hardened and stood about in groups, wearing cloth caps and smoking or chewing strong tobacco. They could cough and spit as well as any man and did so as frequently.

The streets were foul and alongside the more light-hearted entertainments such as buskers and barrel organs, there were dancing bears, cruelly and wilfully mistreated and suffering unspeakable agonies. Stray, starving dogs cowered in the shadows whilst pickpockets would hang around pub doorways ready to fleece the senseless inebriated. The famous Goose Fair attracted travelling thieves in their hundreds and they would gather in the area and fill the lodging houses and furnished rooms, some of which were little more than hovels. In backrooms of the pubs illegal abortionists terminated the lives of the unborn and, by using filthy, primitive instruments (such as crochet hooks) were often responsible for the deaths of the desperate women who sought their services. Those who survived the ordeal were likely to be maimed for life. Barefoot, unkempt children were felons – uneducated maybe, but not lacking in artfulness.

One of the more colourful characters of the area was a notorious criminal, a murdering villain by the name of Charles Peace, who lived in the district for short periods. He apparently had a lady friend there, a Mrs. Hunt. He made his way there on one occasion when he was being pursued by Yorkshire Police and narrowly escaped capture by the local force at a house on the corner of Red Lion Street. The officers discovered Charles in bed and he is reputed to have said, "It's a fair cop, the game's up. I'll come quietly, but for the sake of decency, stay the other side of the door while I dress." They thought this a reasonable request but gave him too long and when they went into the room after him, found it empty, with the casement swinging open. When they ran to the window and looked out, Charles was briefly glimpsed at the bottom of the drainpipe but he got clean away –

the warren-like network of narrow alleys assisting him in his escape and no amount of blowing on the whistle was of any use whatsoever. He most probably made for one of the many caves, some of which housed the performing bears. To search that part would be like looking for the proverbial needle in a haystack. After that, the police learned never to leave their quarry alone again – dressed or undressed.

Both live and stillbirths took place in the grime and filth of the dark alleyways and often the sickly, mewling infants who managed to draw breath were simply abandoned to their fate. Births and deaths such as these were obviously never recorded, but the child mortality rate was anyway very high, and large numbers of babies and very young children simply suffocated whilst in bed with their mothers, at any age from two or three days to six months. It was common for five or six children to share a bed with their parents and indeed many families lived, ate and slept in one fetid room. As might be expected, rats were rife and made their nests in beds where people were sleeping. Much of the area had been demolished by the early 1930s and the goings-on consigned to history, but a more sinister place of ill repute would be difficult to imagine.

Baby Barbara at least was spared the stigma of being born in such indescribable squalor, but what pattern was her life to follow? What was to be the destiny of this innocent, vulnerable, dependent child? That same child who 'went missing' and apparently vanished from the face of the earth almost in the same instant that she claimed her place on it? What happened to her? Could that child have been me?

The baby girl who had just come into the world at 30 Cross Street, approximately 130 miles north west from Downing Street, was to discover in adulthood that her birth certificate was fraudulent and as a direct result of that criminal deception, she was to spend the rest of her life, not like Mr. Bonar-Law, 'The

19

Unknown Prime Minister', but as 'An Unknown Person'. That child is now in her eighties. Until she was in her forties she believed that she was Barbara Hall. She married as Miss Barbara Hall and became Mrs. Barbara Worrall, but twenty-two years and six children later she discovered that when she married, she had actually been somebody else. Barbara Shaw. She had unknowingly been living a lie for all those years. Her marriage was declared invalid; therefore her children were illegitimate. Barbara Hall/Shaw/Worrall had no idea who she was then and is no nearer to the truth today.

During her life, she has been issued with no fewer than seven National Insurance numbers, at least five differing NHS numbers have been assigned to her and even the ID number (RMCU74/4) issued to her during the war appears to have been 'pulled out of the air', as it bore no reference to any personal or family circumstances. Which number can be proved to be valid? Are any of them valid? She has changed her name by deed poll and a legal document states that she is now known by her chosen name of Jane Doe. But who is she really?

I am Jane Doe. I have in my possession the document which, according to the law of the land, states that I am that person. On paper. But who was I in 1923, on 20th May when I was born? Who was Robert Mark Shaw? There are no records to prove that he ever existed. Violet Shaw, apparently, had once been briefly married to a Sydney Shaw. Who was he? Again, there are no records to prove or disprove his existence. And what has been one of the most frustrating aspects of trying to unravel this mystery, and the most soul-destroying? To be met at each and every turn with comments such as, "Sorry, our records do not go that far back", "Sorry, those records have been destroyed" (by fire/flood/other means), "Sorry, we are not at liberty to divulge that information", "Sorry…"

Yes. I am sorry, too, but my sorrow is real and it hurts and it is still festering somewhere deep inside me. Whether acting upon orders or merely indifferent to human feelings, those officials had no idea of the stress and trauma I suffered and will continue to suffer until I know the truth surrounding the birth of Barbara Shaw on Whit Sunday, 1923.

Was I really that child?

Chapter 3   Reunion

I have chosen to begin my story in October of 1967, when I was forty-four years old. For me, this was when my life began. Until that point, I had merely existed, suffering years of torment in the forms of derision, belittlement, physical and mental abuse and duplicity.

But now I was about to embark on a very different journey through life with a warm, caring, human being. For the first time in my life, approaching middle age, I was about to experience true love, something that had been denied me throughout my childhood and all the ensuing years.

It was in the Mecca Bingo Hall during the Indian summer of 1967 that my life began to change. Just before the interval, a group of high-spirited women sitting nearby were making their presence felt. Glancing across at them, I noticed a dark haired man sitting in their midst. Maybe it was the hair, or perhaps his mischievous smile, but I instantly recognised him, even though it must have been at least twenty years since we last met. Catching his eye, I waved and, perhaps boldly for me, beckoned to him. It looked as though they were all sharing a very funny joke, but I could see that he knew who I was and, excusing himself from the merrymakers, he left their chatter. A couple of strides brought him across the aisle to where I sat. He was smartly dressed and his tall, slim frame moved in a relaxed and easy manner.

"You're Cyril, aren't you?" I asked him.

"Yes, that's right." It's Barbara, isn't it? I would know you anywhere, even after…what, twenty odd years, is it?"

I smiled, recollecting our younger days. "I recognised you straight away, even though you were one of twins."

Cyril Clements shook my hand warmly and sat down next to me and we chatted for some time about the days when, as school friends, his older sister, Eileen and I would bath the young twin boys and put them to bed. To me, it was amazing to meet up with him again and it gave me a lovely warm feeling. Cyril told me that he liked to be known as Clem. He revealed that he had recently left his wife after fourteen years of marriage. They had not been getting on very well and, in any case, Marlene was being unfaithful to him. He'd had enough of her antics and had left her to get on with it.

I told him that I had been married to George Worrall for twenty-two years and he was surprised to learn that we'd had six children - Shirley, George, Bonny, Tina, Carol and Mandy the youngest, who was almost five years old. Clem told me he wouldn't have guessed that I was a mother of six because I looked too slim and attractive. My innate modesty prevented me from displaying any pride or vanity, but I will admit that I felt secretly flattered by his comments. My husband was not particularly demonstrative or complimentary and it did feel good to be noticed and appreciated by the opposite sex again. I was well aware that, being petite, with blue eyes and naturally blonde hair, I could still turn men's heads. This was not something I exploited but, as any woman knows, it was reassuring to have confirmation of my attractiveness and Clem boosted my confidence considerably that night.

We went out for a drink in the popular Curzon Arms during the interval and when we returned, I collected three bingo cards for Clem. His luck was in and he won £100. This unexpected good fortune seemed to me to bode well for the future and indeed, I now look back on that meeting as something that was not down to mere coincidence, or chance, but had been securely woven into the gossamer threads that made up our destiny. That weekend was to set the seal on a long and loving relationship that neither of us could have even dreamt about.

When, reluctantly, we parted company at the end of that evening, we had already established a relaxed and close friendship and we felt happy in each other's company. Clem is a very sensitive man and before we said goodnight, he asked me if something was wrong.

"No", I replied. "Why do you ask?"

He told me then that he had noticed sadness in my eyes (the windows of the soul), that he could detect a terrible hurt deep within me. At first, I tried to shrug it off as nothing, but it was no use. I knew that this man was no fool. I also felt instinctively that I could trust him with the innermost secrets that I guarded so closely. Secrets that disturbed my peace of mind.

In fact, as will be revealed during our journey through these chapters, I did have monumental difficulties to grapple with, but the big worry of the moment was that Bonny, my fifteen year old daughter, had run away with a friend to go and work in a pencil factory in Kings Lynn. I planned to go on the bus the following day to see if I could find them. When I told Clem about this, he gently took my hand and said he would help me to go and look for them.

Next morning, Saturday, my husband took me to the bus station and found out which bus I needed to take me to Kings Lynn. Clem had arranged to wait for me so that George wouldn't see him. Eventually I managed to persuade George not to wait for the bus to come and as soon as he was out of sight, Clem came across to me and led the way to a car that he had hired for the occasion. He was a patient, practical man and I felt safe with him at my side.

Our journey to Norfolk was pleasant enough and we chattered happily together, relaxed in each other's company. Once in the town of Kings Lynn, a few enquiries soon led us to where the runaways were staying. It was a decent, clean house and Bonny and her friend Lesley had come to no harm and in fact seemed to be doing all right for themselves. They had their heads screwed on and gave me no reason to worry about them and, in any case, if I had insisted on them coming back with us, I knew they would only be off again somewhere else in a very short time.

We all spent some time together quite cheerfully and finished up on Hunstanton beach which, I remember, was teeming with mussels. We bought ice creams – the expensive kind with a Cadbury's Flake in the top - and sat on a bench enjoying them in the early autumn sunshine before saying our goodbyes and heading back home. I looked in my purse and gave the girls some pocket money, then kissed them goodbye with the customary motherly advice to take care of themselves and keep out of trouble.

This day out had given Clem and me the opportunity to get to know each other better. We felt at ease and comfortable. About half way home, Clem suddenly said, "Barbara, it's been a long day. What do you think of stopping for bed and breakfast somewhere?" I told him that if he thought it was a good idea, it was fine with me, thinking to myself that I would be happier in Clem's company than going back home to George. I knew he would see to the kids, I had no worries there – he may not have been an adoring husband but he was a responsible father.

About a mile or so further on, we spotted a Bed & Breakfast sign and Clem left me in the car whilst he went to make enquiries. He soon came back, and spoke to me through the open car window.

"They can put us up, but they've only a double room. I did ask for two singles, or even a twin-bedded, but the only room available has got a double bed." He looked into my eyes. "What do you think?"

Without any hesitation, I said, "Well let's go and see about it!" I seemed to have shed my inhibitions. I felt emboldened, somehow, and wanted to seize every opportunity as there might not be many more. I felt that our relationship had taken on another dimension. I also knew that I was falling in love with Clem, and the idea of having to share a double bed with him was not only perfectly acceptable, but also very natural. Nobody else mattered to me at that moment.

That night was so special and I treasure the memory of it to this day. I didn't say anything to Clem at the time - I suppose I was a little afraid of scaring him off, after all I was a married woman with responsibilities - but I realised then that I wanted to spend the rest of my life with him. I hoped and wished with all my heart that he felt the same and sensed that he did, but I was too afraid of spoiling the dream to mention anything about it.

After breakfast we settled the bill, Clem left a ten shilling note on the dressing table, (which was a princely tip in 1967), and we made our way back to Nottingham. I was a reluctant traveller that day, in no hurry to break the spell. With the dawn, a few mist patches had settled across the Norfolk Flats and there was a nip in the air first thing, but it promised to be another warm autumn day. By the time we reached Clem's flat, it was indeed gloriously sunny.

"It seems a shame to stay indoors on a day like this, Barbara; we ought to make the most of it". Clem was looking up at the near cloudless sky. "I've had an idea". Then he told me that he would like to take me to a special place as a treat, to round off our weekend together. Well, Clem had the hire of the car until the following morning and George would presume that I had stayed on in Kings Lynn. I could see no harm in our spending the rest of the day together, and I have to confess that I needed no persuading at all. Then I had to play guessing games, trying to imagine where this delightful place was, until I was unable to contain my curiosity any longer.

"Come on, where exactly are you taking me?" I asked, as we set off again, this time in a southerly direction. His captivating smile lit up his face. He was very relaxed and clearly also enjoying the moment.

"To the Derbyshire Dales - you'll love it", he replied.

Love it? That day was the most magical in my entire life. We visited Monsall Dale. As a child, I had roamed the countryside at random in a caravan with a gypsy family, but I had never been encouraged to observe and appreciate the real beauty of the countryside, and this dream of a place literally took my breath away. We were bathed in golden autumn sunshine, the water seemed to sing and laugh with us as it flowed past, carefree, sparkling like diamonds in the sunlight – it was a kind of bejewelled sonata.

I was simply overwhelmed, not only by the beauty of the place, but also by the day itself. Words could not express my feelings and as I held Clem's hand, tears of happiness rolled down my face. It was one of those exquisite, dream-like moments that make you pinch yourself; that you wish would go on forever. I will never forget it, because I know that it influenced my decision to do what I did the following day.

But that day in the dales had been perfect. We left before darkness fell and had a meal in a friendly pub on the way back. Then we rounded off the day at the bingo hall and afterwards Clem took me as close to my home on the Broxtowe Estate as he dared, taking care that we were not seen together. As we kissed goodnight, I felt no guilt or remorse about the fact that I had fallen deeply in love with Clem. I knew only that I wanted to be with him always.

That night found me restless and sleepless. I considered my present existence. I was just being taken for granted. I was always there to cook, clean, do the washing, fulfil marital obligations, etc. But where was the zest in my life? What was there for me to look forward to? I rarely received even a word of thanks from any of the family. They only missed me if I wasn't there to soothe a bruise or patch a knee. They expected food to be on the table and their beds made. My enchanting day out with Clem had made me realise what I had been missing - and what I wanted more of. Then there was the shameful secret I was hiding from them all. Sooner or later that would have to be faced and dealt with; the burden of it was becoming intolerable.

I must have dozed a bit. When I awoke the house was busy with Monday morning activities. Work, school, nursery, sandwiches, shoelaces, hair ribbons, the clatter and rattle of family life. My head was spinning, bursting with thoughts that would not go away. When everyone had left and the house became quiet again, I finally made my decision.

Getting up from the kitchen table, I rinsed the breakfast dishes under the hot tap and left them to drain. Then I went upstairs and gathered a few items of clothing together and some personal bits and pieces. It took me only a few minutes. Hastily tearing a page from the back of a school exercise book, I found a pen and scribbled a note.

"I'm leaving. I've had enough. Don't come looking for me. Barbara."

Taking my door key from my purse, I laid it on the kitchen table on top of the note. Then without a backward glance, I went out into the street, pulled the door securely behind me and walked to the bus stop.

As the bus threaded its way through the busy streets on that Monday morning, I sat staring out through the windows at the people going about their daily business. How many of them had to live with unwholesome mysteries that would not let them rest? I had no idea where I would be in a few hours time, in a flat or hostel or on the streets? I had just made myself homeless but I knew that wherever I ended up, these skeletons from the past would never stop rattling and leave me in peace.

My stop came at last and, leaving the muggy, smoky atmosphere of the bus, I stepped onto the pavement and inhaled the cool, fresh air. "Here goes, Barbara", I told myself as I made my way to number 72, Stratford Road. I had no idea what kind of reception I was going to get, but it was a risk I had to take. Clem's Indian landlord answered my knock on the door. We had already met a couple of times and he knew that Clem and I were close friends so he was quite happy to let me in. It was a little after midday and the quiet street was soaking up the best of the autumn sunshine before the weather broke.

"Clem will be still at work", he pointed out.

"Yes", I agreed. "I know he won't be home until later but I'm sure he won't mind if I wait for him."

The landlord, with a dazzling white smile, showed me up to Clem's flat.

"Smell my wife's most delicious curry", he grinned. "It will give you very good appetite, yes?"

The tiny flat was directly above the Indian couple's home and I remembered Clem remarking that it was impossible to avoid the smell of their cooking, but, as I am well qualified to testify, there are worse things in life to contend with and it was not a problem to me at all. Thinking about food, however, I knew that Clem often made do with fish and chips for supper. After a tiring day cleaning windows, he was usually hungry and understandably had little inclination to start cooking a meal for himself. An idea came into my mind. I went downstairs again and found the landlord busily sweeping leaves away from the front door.

"I'd like to do a bit of shopping", I told him. "Will you be here to let me in again?"

"Oh, yes. Yes indeed". Pausing in his work, he displayed again his very white, even teeth. His smile really was captivating.

"I will be here, my dear. You will find some very good shops down there just round the corner past the trees", he waved his broom cheerily towards the end of the street and continued with his sweeping, still smiling serenely.

When I returned to the flat, I emptied the contents of my shopping bag onto the table. A large lamb chop, carrots and peas and a few new potatoes would make a tasty, nourishing meal for a hardworking man.

I made myself a cup of tea and sat down for a few minutes to drink it before I set about tidying the flat up. Clem kept everything clean - there were no dirty dishes or unwashed laundry strewn about - but it lacked a woman's touch and I enjoyed going round busily tidying up, straightening covers and cushions and putting newspapers away.

Clem usually came home from work around 4.30. At the time he had the contract to clean all the windows at the Loughborough College of Technology. I thought of him coming in tired and hungry, and tried to visualise his face when he realized what was happening. I desperately hoped he would approve. I was counting on staying here at the flat with him now that I had burnt my boats at home. He might not want me there, of course. He had showered me with love and affection since we had met up again, but that was no guarantee that he wanted me living in.

With a shrug, I told myself there was a meal to be prepared and I looked out the saucepans and utensils I would need and busied my hands and mind with the job in hand.

A little before five o'clock, I heard voices below, then footsteps on the stairs and looked towards the door with bated breath, as Clem's key turned in the lock. My heart fell with a sickening thud into my boots when the door was violently swung open and I saw his face wearing an expression like thunder. It was plain that he was furious.

"What the...!" He stopped dead. His expression changed from fury to surprise. "Barbara! What the hell are you doing here? Have you been chucked out?" He held his arms out to me and I rushed into them, colander and all.

"I've come to look after you if you'll have me", I told him.

"Oh, Barbara, there's nothing I want more". Clem hugged and kissed me and my deep sigh was a mixture of relief and great contentment. His initial anger had been due to the fact that his landlord had told him a woman was waiting for him in his flat and he instantly thought that his wife, Marlene, had traced him and was about to stir up trouble for him.

I was on cloud nine. I had come to the end of the old winding road and was about to set off on a new journey. One which was to prove difficult and, hazardous at times but, which I would be able to face, now that I had my soul mate at my side. Without his love and support, I know I could not have coped with the immense difficulties that were heading my way – problems relating to my birth, waiting to blight my life at every turn.

Chapter 4   Who Was My Father?

My earliest memories are of the days I spent as a happy little girl in a tiny cottage in a Hertfordshire village. I can still just remember the idyllic little world I lived in at Roxley Cottages, Willian, with the couple I thought were my parents – the Watsons. The lady I called 'Mummy' was very kind and caring and as there were no other children in the house she was able to devote a great deal of time and attention to my needs and I loved her dearly. One bright, warm spring day, when I was nearly five years old, my safe, sheltered little world came crashing down around me, and splintered my young life with many sharp and wounding fragments. It is truthful to say that I still bear the scars to this day – and always will.

Amusing myself in the small back room with one of my brightly painted wooden toys, I heard a knock come on the door. Mother's footsteps went hurrying down the little passageway of the cottage to open the door, and then the strange voices carried down to the room where I was playing. Mother's voice was soft and gentle - almost musical, and in complete contrast I could hear two other loud, rough voices that I did not recognise at all. One was the deep growl of a man; the other, a woman's, was an odd, rasping kind of drawl. I sat quietly, trying to catch what was being said at the doorstep, when suddenly Mother burst into the room, startling me. Tears were streaming down her face and I felt very apprehensive as she knelt down and hugged me tightly to her, kissing my hair, and sobbing.

"Your... your real parents have come to claim you, Barbara". Barely able to speak, Mother wiped away her tears with knuckled fingers.

"You must go with them, they are waiting", she whispered, releasing me and then blowing her nose hard into an embroidered hanky drawn from her apron pocket.

I was bewildered. I naturally thought that the people I lived with were my real parents. In tears myself by now and very frightened, I snatched up my favourite toy and all my life savings (about two shillings, as I remember) from the money box that the man I called 'Daddy' had made for me from an empty mustard tin. I was very timid in the presence of strangers and peered cautiously round the door to take a look at these new parents of mine, I hadn't liked the sound of the woman's voice and immediately decided that I didn't like the look of the owner of it either, or the man for that matter. They were gypsies and had a strange smell about them, of wood smoke and horses.

I didn't want to go with them and looked up earnestly into my mother's face, willing her to send these two horrid people away. But she again knelt down and, holding me so tightly it almost hurt, she whispered, "Be a good girl, Barbara. You must go with them, they are your parents and there is nothing I can do about it." I was so upset I began to scream blue murder and almost made myself physically sick. Then, still crying bitterly, I wanted to collect a few belongings, but they said there was no room, because my new home was going to be in the oppressive confines of a "Varda" wagon. I knew I would hate it. The cottage was all I had ever known, with the pretty little back bedroom where I slept so snugly in my own little feather bed. I could see the village pond from the window, and the graceful willows bending low to meet their own ghostly reflections in the water. Sometimes, I would look out at dusk and imagine all kinds of wonderful things that might be going to happen down there in the magical hours after dark when little girls were fast asleep. I loved that pond and was often taken across there to feed the ducks.

There had been a family of eight fluffy little ducklings that spring and they had fascinated me with their antics, bobbing about on the surface of the water and waddling so comically behind their parents on the bank. Now I should never see them grow up and produce their own babies next spring.

Apart from the clothes I was wearing – a cotton summer dress, I did take one favourite toy, the little monkey on a stick, which I had been given for Christmas the previous year. Before I left, I managed to persuade them that I needed to visit the 'privy' at the bottom of the garden. While I was in there, I hid the money I had saved - pennies and halfpennies from running small errands for Mother, a sixpence, and a three-penny bit or two. My five-year-old mind told me I would need it when I came back. Some instinct was also warning me that taking it with me would be the same as throwing it as far as I could into the depths of the duck pond.

Having secreted the coins beneath the old wooden toilet seat, I closed the rickety blue door with the gaps top and bottom that let the rain and cold wind in, and promised myself that one day I would be back to collect them (and return I did, but not for another sixty-nine years). Then I walked as slowly as I could, back to the house, with my head bowed and shoulders drooping - a very, very, broken little girl. From that moment on, my life would never be the same again. It was to unfold before me as a living nightmare.

Clutching my faithful old toy monkey on a stick, I went, against my will and still crying quietly, down the garden path with the gypsies, pausing at the gate to take a last mental photograph of the beloved, tranquil place I had known as home. Then I was bundled unceremoniously up the two wooden steps of the "Varda" wagon. This type of home was in its last flourish in the 1920s. It was like one of the gaily-painted caravans featured in the novels of Charles Dickens, and soon to be superseded by the petrol-driven equivalent. This particular wagon had a molliecroft - a raised glass extension above the main body. This was only for the 'better class' gypsy and was expensive. Inside the "Varda" was Lily, who was apparently my half-sister. She was scowling like a bear with toothache and kicked out at me in a jealous rage, hissing venomously, "These are my parents, not yours!"

The woman said I was never to call her mother, but Violet, in public. She was quite small in stature but more than made up for it with her big, loud mouth. She was often very abusive and intimidating. Character wise she was extremely selfish and a very vain individual. The man, tall, spare and olive-skinned, was called Robert. Robert Mark Hall. He said he was my father and I was his daughter, Barbara Hall. My name was Barbara then, and, although I have used a number of surnames since, I remained Barbara until 1995 when I decided to change my name by Deed Poll, and legally became Jane Doe.

Two years of roaming the countryside followed the traumatic episode at Roxley Cottages, Dolly the horse, pulled the wagon, accompanied by Teddy, the Airedale. I loved that dog. He was the only member of the family to show me any genuine, unconditional affection and, like me; he often had a beating for no reason other than just being there.

As a family, we travelled from area to area, clip-clopping along the highways and by-ways, and we found casual work as we went, picking hops and peas. Sometimes, especially in small towns, we would be made to beg in the market squares. This was thoroughly degrading and objectionable and, even at the tender age of five or six; I instinctively felt the shame and indignity of it. Violet used to make paper flowers and carve pegs from the willows and she would give both of us girls a basket to take to sell door to door in the villages. My looks always caused people to make remarks because I was a blue-eyed blonde and they would say, "A fair haired gypsy girl?!" I longed to tell them that I was not a gypsy girl, that these people had stolen me from my parents, but I was too frightened to say anything and I knew I would get a beating from Violet if I dared to open my mouth.

There was a regular visitor to the caravan and, later on when the family had given up life on the road, he would visit the house where we lived in Nottingham. He held the same name, Hall, but was obviously of a different class to the gypsy family with whom he graced his presence. He was a gentleman, a very rich gentleman, according to the money he handed over regularly to Violet, and the expensive presents he showered on me. He would take me upon his knee and say such things as "You are my best girl", and "How is my little Lady Barbara today?" A tall, fair-haired man with glasses and tailored suits, he treated me very tenderly and lovingly and I often wondered who he was. I never got a satisfactory answer and became very puzzled. I was completely flummoxed by these visits.

Why should this charming man come to visit me and bring such beautiful gifts? At length, Violet did tell me that he was Henry Hall, the famous bandleader who was conductor of the BBC Dance Orchestra, which of course meant very little to me, at that time a child of the road. But knowing that somebody famous came to visit me and called me a lady naturally made me feel very special and I wanted to know more about him, and why he came.

"'Henry Hall' famous? Why does he come here, then?" This impudent curiosity had to be discouraged and was met with a sharp "Mind your business and leave it alone!" from Violet's acid tongue. Sometimes the vitriolic outburst would be accompanied by a couple of angry slaps around my ears. Much later, when seeking to put together the jigsaw puzzle that my life had become, I discovered that the famous bandleader was Henry Robert Hall and my so-called father was Robert Mark Hall. It was also revealed that Henry Hall's money had provided the family with the posh "Varda" with its molliecroft and trimmings, as well as the horse and the dog. Was he related to the gypsies? What was his special interest in 'Lady Barbara'? Could he have been my father? Was he a go-between for another even more famous person? Questions, more questions and, no answers; where did these pieces slot into the puzzle?

Those early days on the road have stayed in my memory for more than eighty years. We seemed to be constantly packing up and moving on, running, dodging, hiding, but from whom. Or what? Selling pegs and flowers became part of my daily routine. I remember that householders were often taken aback when they opened the door to two gypsy girls, one of whom was a blue-eyed blonde! Whether it was because of my English Rose looks, I do not know, but I always sold more than Lily and then had to help my dark haired, spiteful half-sister to sell hers. We didn't dare go home until everything was sold and although Lily could make my life unbearable at times with her lies and tale telling, she suffered just as much physical abuse from her mother as I did. There was one memorable incident concerning a farm where we had been working as pea-pickers. The family was about to move on again and one afternoon, Lily and I were ordered to go back to the field and pick enough peas for our evening meal and some to take with us on the road. The pickers would all have gone home, we were told, and we could go and help ourselves. Sure enough, the field was deserted and Lily and I got cracking and had soon picked enough fresh peas to last a few days. We were just ducking under the wire fence, skirts bulging with peas in the pod, when a stern voice called out,

"And what might you two be doing?"

Horrified, we dropped the peas and ran like the wind, back to the "Varda" as fast as we could. We had barely scrambled in, breathless and scared out of our wits, when a loud knocking came on the door. It was the local bobby who, after delivering a forceful lecture on the subject of thieving gypsies

37

(political correctness and racial harassment were unheard of then), agreed that as we had not actually taken the peas away from the field, he would overlook it, but if we were ever caught again, there would be serious consequences. But of course, we still had to face the music from Violet and received two beatings apiece – one for getting caught and one for coming home empty-handed!

Chapter 5   Early Life

To outsiders, we appeared to be a close-knit and loving family, although nothing could have been further from the truth. It also seemed strange that our family didn't mix with other gypsy families despite the fact that we were supposed to be Romanies. Sometimes we would stop off at workhouses during our travels. There would be a welcoming fire and tasty, hot soup with thick chunks of bread, which we would all sit down at long tables to eat.

We travelled to Wales and one village had dark, poky little houses set into the rocks. I was astonished to see chickens and sheep wandering into the rooms from outside, clearly quite at home in these cave-like dwellings. From the Welsh hills, we threaded our way through some enchanting landscapes and found ourselves in Great Malvern, another landmark famous for its hills, in Worcestershire. The weather was atrocious and we stayed for a night or two at a lodging house. It was literally at the side of a quarry which was fenced off, and there were Keep Out notices warning us not to venture beyond the fence.

This was the place where Violet was known and everyone greeted her like an old friend; she knew them all. There was a huge common-room where a welcoming log fire blazed in an enormous fireplace, the like of which I had never seen before. I can still conjure up the crackling warmth from that huge hearth today. There was a long table, the length of the room, where old men and women were sitting, all eating the staple food of soup and dipping their bread into it. Some of them turned round and gave us toothless grins – it was just like a scene from a Dickens novel. Then at bedtime we all slept separately in tiny cubicles right at the top of the house. It was quite a memorable place and I suppose all the more so when I call to mind an incident that was so typical of Violet, bearing in mind her attitude to Lily and me.

One of the women sheltering at the house came over to Violet supporting a very swollen wrist with her good hand.

"Oh Vi, have a look at my wrist will you? It's that painful I don't know what to do with it."

I was at Violet's side at the time and had to witness what followed. Lily had disappeared, sent to bed. Not for any misdemeanour, but she had arrived at the lodging house complaining of toothache and screaming with pain.

"Oh, you'll be alright, go and sleep it off!"

She had more concern for the woman than for her own daughter, but of course this was Violet's character and, we were used to her rough, unloving ways. "Go and sit down. I'll fetch something for you to bite on," was Violet's matter of fact response to the painful wrist.

Coming back with some kind of tightly rolled up cloth; she pushed this into the unfortunate woman's mouth and then proceeded to deal with the problem. The wrist was extremely swollen and inflamed. It was hot and shiny, and I have since discovered that it was most probably what was known as a carbuncle. I do not know exactly what Violet did, but she must have lanced the swelling with some kind of make-do instrument. What I do recall is that the woman suddenly let out a stifled scream of agony and then there was a great deal of green and yellow pus, which smelt as vile as it looked.

I think the two women then cleaned and washed the wound, which was now a huge hole in the wrist and the woman thanked Violet profusely, telling her what a treasure she was and praising her healing skills. I found all this rather strange, considering she would never consider employing the said skills on her daughters, or even take us to a doctor or hospital if we became ill or injured.

I am not sure how long we stayed in the Malvern Hills, or where we went to from there. I know that we passed through some very picturesque towns and villages on our travels, but none of this recompensed me for the squalid life I was forced to live with these people who professed to be my family and took control of my life. It is all behind me now and I am loved and safe and cared for but I will never escape from my past.

Violet could never be bothered to get breakfast for us; in fact she was hardly ever up to see us off to school on the occasions when we did attend. We would have a bowl of thick porridge that Robert had prepared and left to cook in the oven overnight. We often left the house chewing on a slice of cold toast, but there was hardly ever a warm drink for us. Robert came in for a lot of bullying from Violet, but he kept himself pretty well under control and, to his credit, hung in there with her until his demise in 1992, just a few weeks after my second bigamous marriage to Clem.

Looking back to those days, I feel no bitterness. Regret, yes. I do regret and at times resent the fact that a normal childhood was denied me, but that is how my life was and despite the traumas which so disfigured and scarred my formative years and the ensuing mental torment, through it all I have managed to keep my dignity and I know that one day, I will be triumphant... when I find out who I really am.

Chapter 6   Physical, Mental And Sexual Abuse

I suppose the bullying commenced the moment I was hauled up into the "Varda" wagon. The first blows I received were from my so-called half-sister, Lily. She immediately turned on me and kicked me viciously, causing painful and colourful bruising. "These are my parents, not yours!" she shouted at me and I shrank at the venom and hatred that came from a little girl just a couple of years older than me. Even today, in my eighties, I can remember the abject misery that I felt. It was bad enough being snatched away from my cosy, safe little abode where I was loved and wanted, but to be treated like an outcast as well, and my life now in the hands and full control of these strange, rough people – it was way beyond what a small child should ever have to tolerate. I was only four years old – nearly five, but I began to wish I could die, that I had never been born. And where exactly was I born, and to whom? It was obviously not an issue when I was four, but as I grew up, it became more important and for many years now it has been my burning desire to find the answers to these and many other unanswered questions.

But for now, I was a little girl lost, trying my best to keep out of the way and out of trouble so that I would not get a beating with a shoe, or belt, or any other handy object. To be fair, the beatings were not always confined to me, when Violet's temper flared; both Lily and I would be beaten black and blue. We had to be kept away from school on numerous occasions because of the black eyes and bruises we sported. Sometimes I tried to be helpful and do some of the domestic chores to please her.

One evening when she had gone out drinking, I decided the sink could do with a good scrub. It was of the old, yellow, stone type, and was looking pretty grimy. I found some salt in the pantry and set about scrubbing it. It took me some time and was hard work, but do you know, by the time I had finished, it was really sparkling and I was proud of my work. When Violet came home, she actually noticed the sink and said what a good girl I was for making it look like new again. Then she discovered that I had used up nearly all the salt from the pantry and gave me the hiding of my life for it. I was so sore that night; I couldn't lie down in bed and had to sit up all night on the sofa. Lily had gone off with some friends that night, so she was the lucky one and I wasn't.

I well remember another time when both Lily and I suffered a beating and the irony of it was that we had Violet's interests at heart – we were saving up to buy her a pinafore for Christmas. We didn't get very much pocket money, but we were saving a farthing here and a halfpenny there, and when it began to mount up we wanted to find a hiding place for it. We kept the money in a biscuit tin and then we hit on the idea of hiding it up the chimney in one of the upstairs rooms. In those days, it was commonplace to have open fireplaces in bedrooms, and we put the tin on a little ledge up the chimneybreast, pleased with ourselves for having the intelligence to think of such a good hideaway.

Anyway, we came home from school one day to find Violet waiting for us, arms folded, and with a face like a thunderstorm about to break.

"Get up them f***ing stairs, you little bastards, NOW!" she screamed at us, pointing a finger towards the stairs as if we didn't know the way. We hadn't a clue what was wrong and Lily and I looked at each other in despair. We were actually quite close at times – especially when we sensed we were about to get beaten up again. Lily was usually cowering more than I was and yet she was two and a half years older than me and, as far as we now know, Violet's rightful, natural daughter.

Apparently, Violet had also been hiding money up the chimney, away from Robert, who would have gambled it away if he'd been able to get his hands on it. Her little packet had fallen down and she had come across our biscuit tin with quite a bit saved up in it by then and swore that we had been taking her money. Well, we didn't have a clue that she hid her money up the chimney as well and, even if we had, we would have been too scared to touch it, but she didn't believe us and went berserk. She took off her shoe and beat us black and blue with it. I have to say that although I was badly marked, Lily came off worse on that occasion – she had shoe marks all over her body and I remember that Violet and Robert were too scared to send us to school for about three weeks in case it got out about her beating us.

Sometimes, Violet would dress me as a boy in shorts and a little round boater hat and I remember a sailor's outfit that I wore quite a lot. I often had to wear boys' boots or clogs. At times I was even called Bobby. I also had to suffer the indignity of having my hair cut off. Robert said to me once, "You know, she didn't really want you because you weren't a boy."

Was that why she didn't love me, I wondered?

Thinking about the boater brings to mind the time when Lily and I went blackberry picking one Sunday afternoon. I think I was about seven or eight years old and Violet had splashed out on new outfits for us both – probably because we were going to be attending school again shortly. We tried our new clothes on – gymslips, blouses even new knickers and shoes and socks and, of course, smart boaters trimmed with coloured ribbon. Well, as it was Sunday, we were allowed to keep our 'best' clothes on, as long as we kept them clean.

Off we ran, as children do, to gather the luscious ripe fruits and, having picked a handful each, suddenly realized that we hadn't brought anything to put them in.

"Put 'em in your hat," said Lily.

Of course, it had to be my hat. Lily wasn't stupid. When we arrived home with stained, sore fingers, nettled legs and scratched arms, not to mention torn clothing, I was the one with the hatful brimming over at the top with moist, ripe blackberries and dripping dark red juice at the bottom from where the squashed overripe ones were leaking. Violet took one look and flew into a rage. With one well-aimed swipe she knocked the hat from my hands, into the air, so that blackberries were flung everywhere. Then I received a beating for my boater, one for the ruination of my new outfit and the promise of another one if I didn't 'get to the floor this minute and clear up that 'f***ing mess.' Lily didn't even offer to help but just sat on her hands on the table, swinging her legs to and fro and watching me with a smug grin on her face. I think she might have suffered a slap or two from Violet for spoiling her shoes, but I certainly took most of the blame, as usual.

I suffered in all sorts of ways because of Lily, but it was mostly mental stress caused by her sly ways and effortless lying. She also caused me endless misery and shame by her unfortunate and regular habit of bedwetting. We had to share a bed and as she used to wet the bed most nights (indeed, she did so until she was in her twenties), I would get a soaking as well and during the times when we were sent to school, none of the other children in my class would play with me or even sit near me because I smelt of Lily's pee. Lily found herself a few playmates. I think she used to tell them that it was I who wet the bed every night and so they all avoided me like the plague and pitied Lily for having to sleep with a smelly, incontinent half-sister.

As if that wasn't enough, I suffered with my ears because they were constantly being battered by Violet. At times one or both would discharge profusely which was a most unpleasant experience for me, apart from the foul smell, which gave the kids another reason to steer clear of me and call me names.

I can clearly remember the Nit Nurse coming to school and finding both Lily and me infested with head lice and in those days, they used a particularly pungent preparation to kill off the nits. There again, Lily would place all the blame on me, saying that I was the one who had picked up the lice and given them to her, naturally. And guess which one of us got the thick ear for being lousy? School days the best of your life? Maybe for most, but certainly not for me!

As a child I hated the night. Having to tolerate Lily's bedwetting and her spitefulness (she would often pull all the bedclothes off me, or try to kick me out of bed) was a challenge in itself, but I was also afraid of the dark and would lie there, rigid with fear, not daring to move. Sometimes I would have nightmares and wake up crying or screaming, begging to have a light on. Most parents in such circumstances would take their child in their arms and comfort them, making them feel safe and settled again, and loved. All that ever came my way was a violent torrent of four-lettered abuse if I was lucky and, more usually, the obligatory ear walloping.

Whereas Violet was ill tempered and violent towards me, I found Robert on the whole to be a kind-natured man. Of course, he had his moments and there were times when he could be almost as scathing as Violet, but when she wasn't about, he was pleasant enough in his attitude to me. However, as I grew up, he began to take more interest in me and when he sometimes put his arm round my shoulder, or affectionately kissed the top of my head, I felt as if he did care for me.

As time went on, there would be occasions when Violet would go out in the evenings, taking Lily with her and leaving me alone with Robert. It soon dawned on me that these outings

46

of theirs were for a purpose. Nothing was ever said, but I am convinced that Violet not only knew what was going on, but that she also encouraged his disgusting behaviour. As soon as they were out of sight, he would lead me upstairs and, making me lie on the bed, he would fondle and pet me, then lie on top of me. I would have been seven or eight years of age when this began. "Don't worry, Barbara", he would whisper. "I won't put it in."

At that age and, not having mixed much at all with other kids, I didn't really have much of a clue what was going on, but I did realise that it was wrong, if only by his furtive and guilty manner. As time went on, these episodes increased in intensity and frequency, eventually becoming a regular occurrence.

Lighting up a cigarette afterwards he would threaten that "If you ever say a word to anybody, you will be the one to suffer, not me. They'll take you away and put you in a home."

I came to dread the times that Violet and Lily went out shopping, or down to the pub to fetch cigarettes for Robert. The worst thing about it was that I knew that what he was doing to me was wrong and yet I was powerless to stop it. I felt trapped and betrayed by the man I had previously thought was on my side.

Once, I remember, when Violet was in one of her rare talkative moods, she told me that she and Dad hadn't slept together for years. This mystified me at the time. I was the one who had to make their bed and I knew they both slept in it. In my naivety, I didn't know that sleeping together was the accepted and commonplace euphemism for sexual activity, or that sleeping in the true sense of the word was all that went on in their bed. So he relied on me to satisfy his needs whilst Violet was pleasuring the men she met in the pub and no doubt being paid for her trouble, either in money or in kind.

These episodes of abuse continued until I was about eleven years old. Then one day I made up my mind that I just couldn't endure it a minute longer and somehow found the moral strength to stand up to him. I refused to co-operate with his degrading behaviour any longer. The abuse stopped and his attitude towards me changed and once again became one of indifference. There was no respect – there had never been any of that, but he appeared to accept his position and apart from the odd outburst probably born of frustration on his part, he didn't bother me sexually again. Sometimes, when I reached my late teens, he would say, "Barbara, why don't you leave home? Your being here is not good for me or to you."

I know that anyone who has suffered this worst kind of abuse will agree that the scars never leave you. Now in my eighties, those feelings of being tainted, used and cheapened have been with me throughout my life. I have been lucky in that the experience did not affect my ability to consummate a loving relationship, but I know that there are many victims whose adult lives have been completely ruined by the selfish and despicable actions of such perverts and bullies.

So there were very few rough edges left on me as I grew into adulthood and one thing I had learned was to keep my mouth shut. Indeed, like the three wise monkeys, I heard it all, saw it all and kept it all to myself. Until now, that is, and the truth, unwholesome and distasteful though some of it may be, can finally be told.

"It is with regret that I have to tell you that England is now at war with Germany". Neville Chamberlain's solemn voice crackled across the airwaves, sending out the chilling news to every British household in possession of a wireless receiver. Those without broadcasting equipment made their way to friends' or neighbours' houses so that they could hear the latest on the grave and growing conflict with Germany. Rumours had been rife for days. When the news finally came through, some were shocked, some had expected it, many just could not believe it, but all had hoped and prayed that the day would never come. Women wept in secret, fearful of the future as their men folk prepared themselves for what turned out to be a bloody and gruesome conflict that lasted for six years.

A very different kind of war was about to be waged in my personal life as a young and vital Barbara Hall, but mine was to continue inexorably throughout my lifetime. Aged just sixteen years and four months when World War II began, two memorable events were to take place in my life before the fighting ceased. Young and innocent, I was blissfully unaware of the devastating turmoil which lay ahead and which would eventually destroy my peace of mind and test my sanity to the limit.

Nearly four weeks on from the declaration of war, in common with the rest of the population, I was issued with a National Identity Card. However, it appeared from the outset to be a fabrication, as the numbers on it seemed to have no connection with me at all. The ID cards were supposed to correspond with details such as the area you came from, your place of birth and the number of siblings you had. The number given to me, RMCU74/4, made no sense whatsoever. Not that I myself was aware of anything being wrong at the time; it was discovered many years later that this had been just one among countless similar instances of being issued with identifying documents which were false and, therefore meaningless. They were also worthless and proved nothing.

There was also considerable conflict relating to my home and family life at this time. From the age of nearly five, when I had been taken from a loving home by gypsies purporting to be my parents, I had suffered all manner of abuse at the hands of both so-called parents and my half-sister, Lily. Now in my mid-teens, I was only too glad of the opportunity to go out and earn a living. For the first time in my life, I was to have a taste of freedom. In common with all wage earners of the day, I was restricted by rules and disciplines of working practice, but at least I was out during the day, enjoying some respite from the oppressive atmosphere at home.

Chapter 7   Barbara's War 1939 – 1945

I was employed at Nottingham Castle, packing air force uniforms. It is very telling that for the duration of my time there, I was never allowed to open my own wage packet. It had to be delivered up to Violet (my so-called mother), who would open it, take out my hard-earned cash and keep it all, just occasionally handing back two shillings for stockings, or whatever, if she happened to feel in a generous mood.

At seventeen, I volunteered for the Land Army and was sent to work at Somer Leyton in Suffolk. At first, I found it very difficult to settle down there. I was a rather timid and reserved teenager, and didn't socialise very much to begin with and I was also very nervous of the cows - well, frightened to death of them, to be honest! However, after a week or so, I did relax a little more and began to enjoy the life but, true to form, my 'family' soon managed to sour things for me.

I had not been there long when a telegram came from my father requesting, "COME HOME AT ONCE STOP VIOLET ILL STOP". This was a typical example of the family disrupting my life. It was always happening and really got me down at times. I very much doubted whether there was any truth in the telegram but felt unable to ignore it, so I packed my kit bag and walked to the station. I had no money as I had not yet been paid, so I had to explain matters to the Station Master, showing him the telegram from home. He took pity on me, saying that he thought I looked very troubled, and he issued me with a warrant to travel. He told me it was wrong that so pretty a young girl should wear such a sad look.

"Cheer up, do," he called out as I boarded the train. "It may never happen!" I was never contacted again by the Land Army - for one thing I had not been recorded as ever being there.

Barbara Hall was not on record. Barbara Hall has never been on record! That is the whole point.

Of course, when I arrived home and, as I had suspected all along, Violet was not ill. She was her normal selfish, greedy self. The Ministry of Defence at Nottingham Castle where I had worked packing uniforms had written, explaining that I had some tax to be refunded amounting to about £20 and, as the Inland Revenue required my signature – a tax rebate was; after all, an official document - only I could claim it. So Violet sent me up there to do just that and then took it from me, leaving me with half a crown in the world to my name and no job. This was a mere fraction of the emotional and mental pain I had endured for twelve years at the hands of this tyrannical family. These deeply wounding episodes have collectively caused me enormous personal stress and had detrimental effects on my mental and physical health.

Shortly after leaving the Land Army, I went to work at Luxfers bomb-filling factory. I had a good job driving the dillies carrying the loaded bombs and had to be issued with a pass as only restricted personnel were allowed in to that area. I remember a cheerful young man of similar age to me called John, with whom I worked. He rode at the back of the dilly and as we drove around with our hazardous cargo, we would be singing the popular wartime songs together. I was still only about eighteen and found myself in a position that demanded responsibility and reliability and I felt quite a sense of pride. I began to gain more self-confidence and extended my interests as I realised that the big world outside of the prison of my home had much to offer. Having tasted freedom, I found it to my liking and, naturally, desired much more of it.

When I was about nineteen, I met a Canadian Petty Officer called Frank Gibbons, and we began to go out together. On one occasion we went to a dance hall in Sheffield and, as it was very late when we came out - past midnight, Frank suggested that we stay overnight in a hotel. I agreed after a bit of discussion, but in any case there didn't seem to be much choice at that time of night – it was no good even thinking about trying to get home and if I had, I would have found myself firmly locked and bolted out. We spent the night in a double bed and I kept most of my clothes on all night.

"Do you always sleep in your clothes, Barbara?" Frank asked me. I couldn't begin to explain. After the abuse I had suffered earlier at the hands of Robert Hall, my so-called father, I was just too frightened to do otherwise. Frank said he wanted to marry me and take me back to Canada when the war was over and even gave me a lovely ring, which had once belonged to his mother. The ring was most unusual - I had never seen one like it and haven't done so since. Set in gold, the stone was like an emblem and changed colour. I was fascinated by it and wore it all the time. One day I took the ring off at home to wash my hands and never saw it again. I knew that Robert had taken it to finance his gambling habit, but I also knew that it was pointless to accuse him, or indeed anyone else in the house, of taking it.

Early in 1945, I met George Worrall, the man who was to become my first husband. He was in the navy. I used to go to a pub called the Foresters Arms Public House with the people I worked with. George had three sisters, Renee, Ivy and Joyce. This particular evening, they all happened to be in the pub with George, and I was having a drink before going on to work on the night shift at Luxfers. One of the sisters invited me to join them. As my mates weren't in that night, I was glad of the company and spent a happy, sociable evening with them. In fact, they persuaded me to take the night off work and I was late home that night and had to sleep in the toilet as I had been locked out.

After that first meeting, George and I began to see each other regularly and in a matter of weeks, he had asked me to marry him. I realised later that he was on the rebound following a broken romance, but at the time I was unaware of this and accepted him immediately, overjoyed at the prospect of not only having someone in my life to love me at last, but also of finally being free from the wretched prison like existence which was all I had known since my childhood days. Little did I realise then that my forthcoming marriage was to be the catalyst for the life sentence I would have to serve.

The first sign of trouble was apparent when I went to publish the Banns. George had just returned from South Africa and his ship was docked at Bristol, but as he was unable to get immediate leave, he asked me if I could take care of the arrangements from Nottingham. I foresaw no problems at all and made my way to the Registry Office in Shakespeare Street and proceeded to give the Registrar our names - Barbara Hall and George Worrall. I was then asked for my birth certificate. "What do you want my birth certificate for?" I enquired, quite innocently. "I am nearly twenty-two years old. In any case, I haven't got a birth certificate". I remember the Registrar looking me up and down two or three times, making me feel very uncomfortable. I was very petite and, I suppose, did look younger than my years.

"You don't look twenty-two. You look very young to me. I must verify your age as well as your identity. I can't proceed until you bring your birth certificate." He clattered shut the heavy book that he had begun to write in, then leaned across the desk and in almost a whisper, added "You had better bring a parent with you." This made me feel perplexed and anxious. It was all going wrong again. When was anything ever going to work out in my favour? I blinked back the hot, stabbing tears.

"But I don't need my parents' consent. I am over twenty-one!"

The registrar was unmoved and insisted that until I returned with my birth certificate and a parent; he could not proceed further with the matter.

When I reached home, Robert and Violet were sitting at the table and ignored my presence, as usual. I was used to being invisible to them most of the time, but when I blurted out, "I am going to get married and I need my birth certificate!" Violet's head jerked round so violently that it was a wonder she didn't sustain a serious neck injury. As for Robert, he shot up from his seat at the table like a startled hare, scraping the chair across the linoleum and upsetting a jug of milk all over the table.

"What did you say - married? Who would want to marry you?" Violet curled her lip and spat the words at me venomously. She then turned her attention to Robert, who had now recovered his composure and stood leaning against the wall, arms folded defensively across his chest.

"Now what are we going to do?" she screeched at him in her rough, rasping voice. "I knew we'd get caught out one day, I knew we would!" Almost hysterical, Violet was violently thumping the table with both fists, making the teacups and saucers rattle and shake about on the milk-sodden lace tablecloth. Robert moved to face Violet and, bending so that their faces were level, he said in a quiet voice, which belied his anxiety.

"Look, there's no need to worry. I'll soon sort this out. I'll go with her and get it settled. It'll be all right - you'll see".

No more time was wasted and I made a second journey to Shakespeare Street, this time accompanied by Robert, and desperately hoping that he had meant it when he said it would be all right. We walked into the office and the Registrar looked up from a desk in the corner.

"Ah, you are back, and this is your father?"

"I am her father", put in Robert before I had a chance to answer for myself. The Registrar, a gaunt, skeletal individual, coughed nervously and breathed on his spectacles, polishing them with a snowy white handkerchief, which he replaced in his breast pocket, before giving me his fish-eye stare.

"Now then, Barbara, I want you to go and sit outside for a few minutes while I, er, just have a few words with your father. It won't take long." He indicated the door with the palm of his hand and I meekly did as he asked and went and sat outside in the corridor. I hadn't really any choice in the matter. I wondered why I was being kept in the dark when, after all, it was me they were discussing, and my business, not Robert and Violet Hall's. What could they be saying about me behind the closed door and behind my back? I sighed deeply. As long as I was still going to be able to continue with my plans and marry George, I didn't really care - after all, if it was bad talk about me, and it probably was, I couldn't hear them. I just wanted to get it all sorted out as quickly as possible.

After about twenty minutes, which to me seemed more like a lifetime, the Registrar came out.

"I am going to let the Banns go ahead", he said. Then, wagging his bony index finger menacingly at me, "But you must promise never to say anything to anyone, or you will get me and your father six months".

I was rather startled by his thinly veiled threat, but didn't really want to think about it at the time. To my mind, the whole episode had been unnecessary and a complete waste of time. All I wanted to do was to get out of there, go to George in Bristol, marry him and lead a new life. But there was more trouble ahead.

On 4th May 1945 I travelled down to Bristol where arrangements were at last in place for us to get married. George was given leave to meet me at Templemead Station. We spent about two hours together, then he booked me into a women's hostel for the night and returned to his ship until the following day - our wedding day.

The lads on board helped George celebrate his last night as a bachelor and helped him into his bunk in the wee small hours. I didn't sleep much that night either. The journey had been tedious and tiring, but I really felt too excited to relax. I was going to be George's wife tomorrow - a married woman. "Mrs. Barbara Worrall". I kept repeating the name to myself. I would have a new name tomorrow - I would be the same Barbara, of course, but with a different identity and at last I would be able to live a normal life. I could not have guessed then how ironic my frivolous girlish thinking would turn out to be.

George and I attracted a few admiring glances as we made our way to the Registry Office the next morning and I felt like the bee's knees. I expect we did stand out rather, and it must have been obvious that we were on our way to tie the knot. I had chosen a green suit, which suited my colouring. George always said he was attracted by my English rose looks. I wore cream accessories and carried a simple posy of spring flowers. George, proverbially tall, dark and handsome was smart in his naval uniform. Passers-by smiled at us, touched probably by our undisguised happiness. However, our joy quickly turned sour when we arrived at the registry office and the Registrar refused to marry us.

"I am very sorry", he explained, "But I cannot marry you. There is nothing recorded for a marriage to take place between Barbara Hall and George Worrall. You have not resided in the district long enough, and Barbara, you have no birth certificate".

I was so shocked, I gasped when he said this. I simply could not believe that this was happening to me again. George glanced at me rather crossly - I had assured him that everything was arranged. What on earth was going on now? Fighting back bitter tears, I explained to the Registrar that these matters had already been dealt with by the Registrar in Nottingham.

"That was Nottingham", he snapped. "This is Bristol". But I was determined that I would not give in. I'd had to overcome so many obstacles to get this far and I was not going to be denied my one chance of happiness now. The thought of having to go back home to Robert and Violet and endure their cruel sarcastic comments was intolerable and made me even more determined to stand up for myself - something which had never come easily to me. But I stood my ground and, after some argument, I eventually persuaded the Registrar to telephone to Nottingham. He grumbled about it all being most irregular and not having the time for all this nonsense, but he did agree to speak to the Nottingham Registry Office, if only to get this pair of nuisances off his back and out of his office. After several minutes, he came back in a huff. Stony-faced, he barked, "Alright. Go and get two witnesses off the street and I will perform the ceremony!"

Three days before VE Day, on 5th May 1945, I began my new life as Barbara Worrall, and for many years it was a good one. I enjoyed being a homemaker and a mother, and took to my new role very easily and naturally, in spite of a miserable childhood spent mostly on the move with a family that was anything but natural. George and I steadily increased our family until there were eight of us. We had six children to care for - five girls and a boy, and I happily accepted and lovingly carried out my responsibilities as a wife and mother.

What was it, then, in 1967 that drove me to walk out on them all, never to return? Why, after twenty-two years of marriage and six children did I make the decision to turn my back on my home and the family that I loved?

Chapter 8   Who Am I?

Clem and I moved into number 2 Chard Street in January 1968. We had acquired the tenancy of the house through my friend Celia whom I had met at the Bingo hall on St Ann's Well Road. She and her husband Dennis lived at number 4 Chard Street. Celia's husband was an expert at embroidery and all kinds of needlework; a true artisan. When we eventually agreed the tenancy with the owner and moved in, I was very reluctant.

Just taking another look at the place suggested I ought to run a mile - and get my head looked at for good measure. The place was a shambles, an absolute mess that needed endless tender loving care. Clem and I had to sit on the floor, as we didn't have a stick of furniture, no pots nor pans, nor any bedding either. We were in total desperation. But after a serious heart-to-heart we decided to try and make a go of things and give it our best shot.

On our first day in our new home we busied ourselves visiting second hand shops to purchase crockery, pots and pans and items of bedding. Then for the next two weeks we slept on the floor, not the best start for us, but we were determined to make it work. Clem set off for work the next day. As a Public Service Vehicle driver with Nottingham City Transport I knew he would be late home. He worked long hours and was always available for overtime and with the extra money we were able to buy additional things for the house. I had managed to persuade the greengrocer to let me have some orange crates, so at least we had something to sit on. With the addition of some cushions and bright covers, it was beginning to look a bit more like a home by the time Clem came in from work.

The house was very old and in a poor state of repair - dilapidated is an understatement. In fact it was earmarked for demolition. It was in a terrace, with covered side entries at four house intervals, allowing access to the rear of the properties. Factories towered at the back of these alleyways, casting shadows into the backyards. It was from the semi-darkness of one of these archways on the opposite side of the street that, unbeknown to us, our comings and goings were being watched. Yes, as will be seen later, we were under surveillance. Again. Although the property was nearly derelict, Clem decided to take on the task of renovating it. This was quite a challenge, especially at that particular time when we were battling to survive financially, work being very spasmodic. There were electricians working at one of the factories to the rear of the house and we asked them how much they would charge to make the place safe to live in. They came up trumps and set about rewiring the house for us. They did an excellent job for £60 and at least we felt safe in that we were no longer in imminent danger of frying in our boots each time we used a socket or light switch.

Clem's hours were very long and tiring. He covered one of the main routes operating out of Parliament Street. But the money was good and before too long we were able to purchase some new furniture. I remember we had a suite comprising a bed-settee and two chairs, a 'dancing flame' electric fire, standard lamp, and wall lights. Clem re-decorated the rooms, mostly in magnolia, which was a popular choice three decades ago and is still, apparently, among the best selling shades. To us, especially after the conditions of Stratford Road, the place slowly became a little palace. Our home-making efforts seemed to set the seal on our relationship and we began to settle into a routine. Clem would go off to work and my days were filled with the busyness of domesticity. These so-called everyday chores were enjoyable activities as far as I was concerned. Keeping our home fresh and bright was a pleasure and, for the first time in my life, I felt valued for myself rather than for the services I could provide.

Above all, to be genuinely loved and cherished and cared for, was the closest thing to heaven that I could ever have imagined.

But despite this newly found contentment, my deep-seated anxieties refused to go away and they surfaced during unguarded moments. They often manifested as full-blown nightmares and on occasions I awoke both of us as I tossed and turned, muttering and sometimes shouting out in my sleep. Most of the time, Clem was unable to understand the jumble of words. He was completely mystified by these strange, unexplained outpourings but in his own mind put it down to the stress of leaving my family and making a challenging fresh start. He showed commendable patience and restraint. Working long, demanding hours as he did, the last thing he wanted was to have his much needed sleep disturbed by my paranoid ramblings. Then one night, which was actually his birthday, the 16th June 1968, he was half awake in the semi-darkness when I was gripped by yet another wild episode. This time I was in a highly emotional state and he was unable to calm me. "Who am I?" I asked him, tears streaming down my face. "For pity's sake, tell me, who am I?"

Clem put the light on and held me close until I stopped shaking. Then, gently holding my face at arm's length and looking into my eyes, he said firmly, "Barbara, time you were straight with me and told me what's been troubling you. I'm not a fool and I've known for a while now that you've been grappling with some kind of demon and if we are to make a go of things, then the first thing is, we've got to be honest with each other. No secrets. Now then, what's going on?" I immediately swung my legs out of bed and crossed the room to fetch my handbag, taking from it a tattered, ink-stained piece of paper. That dog-eared document more precious to me than gold, even though I hated with all my heart the words that were inscribed

upon it. It was my birth certificate. Or was it? I handed it to
Clem.

"This," I said, "is what is troubling me and has been for
about two years now. This is why I walked out on my family
without warning or explanation, because I did not know how to
live with the guilt and the shame!"

And yet I had done nothing to warrant such remorse.

I began to tell Clem the whole story, which, as far as I
know, started on 20th May 1923. Whit Sunday when Stanley
Baldwin became British Prime Minister. The day I was born. But
what took place between that date and the spring day some five
years later when I was taken from my loving home in a
Hertfordshire village by gypsies, I will never know. Clem and I
have spent half a lifetime trying to get at the truth about my birth
and the reasons behind the despicable, deceitful bureaucracy we
have encountered at every turn.

Many times I had wanted to tell Clem all about my
mysterious past and the bizarre circumstances surrounding my
discovery that I was not Barbara Hall, and never was or ever
could be. I just never seemed to be able to find the right moment
to raise the subject. I knew I couldn't go on keeping it bottled up
and if I were to spend the rest of my life with Clem, as I prayed I
would, then he had the right to know. When, finally, that night I
was able to take the first step, I found that I was able to open my
heart to him and no-one could possibly imagine the immensity
of the relief that I felt when Clem said that he understood how I
must feel and not only that, but also that he would always take
care of me and pledged there and then to do his utmost to help
me find some answers. That was the moment when I knew I
would never feel lonely or unloved again and I also believe that I
was pulled back from the brink of insanity by that realisation.

Chapter 9   Naming Our Child

Clem and I faced insurmountable problems when registering Darran's birth. As far as I was concerned, the child was a miracle anyway, considering the fact that I had been sterilized in 1964 following the birth of my youngest daughter. It seemed it was also going to take a miracle to satisfactorily register his birth. As Darran's mother, was I to identify myself as Barbara Hall (maiden name), or Barbara Shaw (birth certificate name) or, even worse, could I be forced to use my married name of Barbara Worrall? After several visits to the registry office, they offered no compromise and we returned home each time with no resolve as to what name our newborn son should take.

We looked at the whole issue of his birth and decided, as I had been estranged from my husband for almost two years, our son should have been registered in my maiden name of Hall, Barbara Hall being the name I gave over in marriage to George Worrall on the 5th May 1945 at the Bristol Registry office. I knew of no other name until I was forty-two years of age when, after my third visit to the registry office, I had finally been handed that mythical document by the superintendent registrar. I will never forget how I rushed outside and walked a short distance from the registry office before opening the document out to discover to my horror that it was for Barbara Shaw and not, as I had expected, for Barbara Hall.

I had always known myself as Barbara Hall. Even throughout my schooling, which was almost non-existent, the family was known as the Halls. I never for one moment dreamt or believed that I could be any other person than Barbara Hall and I carried the name well. At the time of our earlier years on the road, we were considered by some to be travelling people. To others we were gypsies. It was a description that I hated and was so glad when we settled at 14 Kelvin Street, Dalton, Rotherham.

This was the place I came to know as Dalton Brook, where my sister Lita was born. Her birth certificate reads, "Violetta, girl 5th July 1929, father Robert Mark Hall (informant), mother Violetta Hall formerly Goss". Could this be the very same person who married Sydney Shaw some ten years earlier in 1919? I don't suppose I'll ever know. I was known as Barbara Hall when I married George Worrall. How did this switch in my life come about? I had suddenly become an unwitting victim to this turn of events and the name of Barbara Shaw on my birth certificate would complicate matters even further.

Clem, as Darran's biological father, naturally wanted him to be registered in his name of Clements. However, when we requested this, we found ourselves in an impossible situation. The terse reply was, "You two are not married." How was it possible for them to know this, we certainly had never notified or advertised that we were not a married couple?

Putting aside for the moment that my ambition in life has always been to verify my identity, our biggest concern at that time was to be able to legitimize the birth of our son. We even discussed not registering him at all, so placing the burden of proof as to my real identity onto the authority that had identified me as Barbara Shaw in the first place, together with my so-called parents Robert Mark and Violet Hall. There must have been certain, privileged other parties who also knew the truth. This had, after all, been a well kept, if not a best kept secret.

To our amazement, in our later endeavours to uncover the truth, we were notified that my birth records were closed to public scrutiny until the year 2038. This has since been amended to 2026. Will I still be around when I am one hundred and three? I am sure the bureaucrats are praying that I won't be. On the copy that we hold it is stated that the records for the midwife, Sarah Ellen Wheatley and her mother Mrs. Barnes are closed until the later date. We have no indication of whether these records relate to Barbara Hall or Barbara Shaw and it is possible that we have now run out of time.

We had certainly run out of time in relation to registering our son's birth and were now facing threats that he would be taken from us and placed into care. We must register him forthwith or face the consequences and we were fully aware of what that meant; we risked losing our love child, he would be put up for adoption and we might never ever see him again. I then wondered if history was repeating itself. Could something like this have been the cause of my false birth records? Unlikely, perhaps. But will we ever know for sure?

My birth certificate, if in fact it is a record of my birth, shows that it was recorded twenty days after I entered this world. In Darran's case we were well and truly past the legal limit of forty-two days in which to register and we were desperate to resolve the situation.

Eight weeks after the delivery of our healthy son by caesarean section, we again attempted to register his birth. We suggested he should be in the name of Hall. The registrar did not approve and this attempt by us to solve the problem was swiftly rejected. We stood our ground that he was not to be named Shaw and suggested the name Clements, which was also rejected. Was there no end to this ordeal? Suddenly the official came up with one way that he could be named Clements. She then turned to me and said, "If you give your child up for adoption," she then faced Clem, "You can then adopt him, Mr. Clements, and that will make it quite legal."

Clem reacted to her suggestion with utter contempt and replied, "That's all very well, but what happens when my son reaches the age of say fourteen and says "Dad are you my real dad?" and I reply that of course I am son, then he replies, if I am your real son, why did you have to adopt me?" We did eventually leave the registry office with a birth certificate for

Darran, having signed the register as Mrs. B. Clements and Mr. C. Clements. My maiden name was entered as Hall but not at the time of registering; it was not until many years later, that I discovered that the registry office had submitted the name Hall onto the certificate. We returned to our humble home at 2, Chard Street with its damp surroundings and wondered how we could have permitted ourselves to bring our young son into a place such as this. All our efforts at homemaking could not prevent the rising damp, which was getting worse. We would have to look to making a move; both Clem and I had suffered pneumonia and Darran was starting with bronchitis. Clem's illness had put him out of work, benefits then were non-existent and we were literally in one hell of a mess.

I tried to reassure Clem that everything would turn out okay but it never did. Then on my return one day from shopping on Hyson Green I noticed an empty house at the corner of Wilkinson Street. I told Clem about it and persuaded him to make enquiries of the owner and shortly afterwards we were given the keys to it. We were refused a moving grant by the Department of Health and Social Security, so for the sum of five pounds loaned to us reluctantly by Clem's elder sister Eileen, the coalman agreed to move us in. The last piece of furniture entered our new home at five minutes to midnight by Shipstones' brewery clock. We were now residents of 345, Radford Road, Hyson Green, Nottingham and this was just one of the very many houses we were to inhabit over the coming years. It was the beginning of our journey along the road that never seemed to lead anywhere. But at least we had each other and our son, and he had a birth certificate that showed the names of his true parents.

Chapter 10   Finding Roxley Cottages

Sixty-nine years after my abduction, we decided to have a serious attempt at finding the cottage where it all took place. On June 19th 1998, three days after Clem's birthday I begged him to take me in search once again of the cottage that I still had such fond memories of and he agreed.

Just after daybreak we drove off down the A1 towards Hitchin and because of the volume of traffic, missed a turning and soon became hopelessly lost. We had somehow found our way onto the M11 and were sixty miles off course. Several hours later as we were heading back again towards Nottingham, I spotted the turn that we had missed. This second visit to find the cottage was to open a minefield of research the likes of which was beyond our wildest dreams. Clem stopped the car. At that moment he was, understandably, not in favour of turning round and tackling the journey again, especially as we didn't really know what to look for. I used all my powers of persuasion on him and eventually got my own way, though I have to admit he was rather reluctant.

So we set off once again for the library in Hitchin where two years previously they had been intrigued by my story in the press and had been anxious to help. Also in response to a newspaper article in the Hitchin Comet the same year, we received a letter from a man who told us that he remembered his mother talking about a child being taken by strangers from the cottage nearest to the village shop. The couple who lived there had been the Watsons and this is borne out by entries in the Letchworth Streets Directory for the relevant period. I became excited because I knew this visit could be vital in providing proof, not only to Clem but also to the rest of the world that my story was not some school girlish fairy tale and I had not dreamt it all up.

Heading in the direction of the library, Clem noticed a village sign: Willian. We had received a letter from another person who had read my story in 1996, saying that they thought, by my description of where I was taken from, that the place could have been Willian. But by the time we noticed the sign we had already passed by and I didn't want Clem to get too fed up with all this as I knew he must be feeling very tired by now, so I told him not to bother going back but just continue on to the library. He didn't say a word, but found a suitable place to turn around and then headed back in the direction of the village. To this day I am so grateful to Clem for doing that, otherwise I would probably have never realized my dream to find the cottage that I had so cruelly been taken from nearly seven decades earlier.

It is difficult to describe my emotions as we took that road leading into the village. I was very fidgety and filled with a kind of awe at the prospect of confronting the scene where I was hoping to find traces of my lost childhood. It was exciting, but at the same time I felt really anxious about it and my insides seemed to be full of butterflies. Clem drove very slowly through the village, hoping that I might spot something that I recognized – any little thing that might jog my memory. Of course, peering through a car window was not the ideal way of looking out for what would now be only vaguely familiar landmarks. The one thing that we were hoping to see was a village pond, but there was no sign of one. The pond, visible from my little bedroom window, had been my best-kept memory over the years, and I knew that if I saw it again, I would know it instantly.

I began to wonder if we even had the right village. There was not much sign of life and so far we had not set eyes on another human being. Clem pulled up at the kerbside, outside a pub.

"Come on, Barbara." He locked the car and put a comforting arm round my shoulder. "Let's go and see what they can tell us in here." There were about half a dozen people inside the pub, chattering as they drank. As we approached the bar, the landlady greeted us, no doubt expecting us to order drinks.

"Can I help you, sir?" She was smiling pleasantly.

Clem said, "I'm hoping so. Does this village have a pond?"

Evidently, to the locals, this must have sounded like a very strange request because everyone stopped talking instantly and absolute silence descended on that lounge bar. Clem and I looked at each other rather awkwardly. Everyone was staring at us and we felt quite embarrassed for having dared to ask what seemed to be a perfectly innocent question. The landlady gave us a very strange look and pointed to the view from the window. "There is a pond over there – where that telegraph pole is."

We thanked her and beat a hasty retreat. The telegraph pole was across the road from where the car was parked and to the left of the pole; we could now see a pond. Evidently the locals had thought we were halfwits, going into the pub to ask where the pond was when it was under our noses! In our defence, I can only say that until we reached the pole, we could not see the pond for the tall grass and weeds growing up in front of it. Neither of us spoke as we walked around the edge of the pond. Clem gave me a breathing space for a few moments to allow me to take it in and try to get my bearings. But, with my heart in my boots, I turned to him in abject disappointment.

"No, Clem. This is not the pond."

Clem also looked downhearted. "Well, you sound very emphatic, Barbara." I felt like crying. I had so much wanted to find the pond, to prove to Clem that this was the place where I had left my childhood behind all those years ago. I desperately wanted it to be that same village pond. But it was not and I couldn't pretend otherwise – not to Clem and certainly not to myself. I felt hopeless and helpless. At that moment, it seemed that I would never be able to prove that this was where it all started, where my life hit the buffers and came off the rails.

Somehow, I managed to stem the flood of tears that I could feel welling up inside, knowing that if I gave way to them I would find myself sobbing uncontrollably – all the pent-up emotions of yesteryear were perilously near the surface. Also, I was conscious of the curiosity we had aroused in the pub and had this uncomfortable feeling that every move we made was now being watched. Purposely, we did not look in that direction. I sat on the fence at the side of the pond. Clem joined me and we sat there together quietly for a while. "Does it stir any memories?" asked Clem, hopefully. I shook my head despondently.

"No. Come on, let's leave it and go to the library." I felt so disillusioned I just wanted to get out of the place. Clem took some photographs of me at the pond and then went back across the road, with me trudging behind him. He suddenly said that he was going to try and locate the oldest inhabitant of the village on the off chance that he or she might be able to give us some clues. This gives you an idea of the kind of man Clem is. He had been driving about the countryside all day, missing turnings and getting lost in all these strange places and after finally locating the place, we were still no nearer to solving anything. He knew how important it was for me to be able to substantiate what I had told him about this very traumatic part of my life and he meant to do all within his power to try to satisfy that longing in me.

There was no response at the first house we tried, but we were in luck next door. A young man answered our knock and listened as Clem explained briefly what we were doing in the village. He was far too young to be of any assistance to us but he did say he would ask around and took our telephone number in case he came across any information. He also advised us not to leave the village without speaking to the Postmaster at the village store, just a little further on up the road from the pub. I was not holding my breath; in fact I thought it was just going to be another waste of time and another let down. But I was so wrong. Our encounter with the Postmaster completely changed the complexion of the matter.

I described the little one-roomed school that I could remember and he suddenly pointed towards a bend in the road. Just round the corner was the very school, he said, but it had been converted into a house now. Clem and I exchanged glances, thanked the Postmaster and hurried away, anxious to find out what lay round the bend.

We hadn't walked far when I suddenly experienced a really strange feeling and stopped. I squeezed Clem's arm tightly. Walking on, I again had to stop for a moment. I cannot explain it, but I seemed to be rooted to the spot. Clem was concerned.

"Are you alright, my love?"

My mood had changed in an instant. No longer was I a dejected, negative Barbara, but a very positive, optimistic one.

"Yes. Oh yes! The cottage I was taken from is on the other side of this hedge. I know it is. "

Clem's anxiety increased. He confessed to me afterwards that he thought I had lost the plot. In a low voice and looking very serious, he said, "Oh now come on Barbara, you can't possibly know that. For a start, the hedge is too thick and too high to be able to know what's behind it."

But something drove me. Ignoring Clem's protests, I took over completely and taking his hand in mine, walked to the lane end where I turned to open a wicket gate and strode through it straight into my past. Here, at last, was the place where I had skipped and sung and played as a happy little girl sixty-nine years ago. There was no emotion; I did not have to prove a thing. I was back, after years of trying to persuade friends and family that I had been speaking the truth from the beginning – and the beginning was right here in front of me. I knew every inch of the place and my heart sang out as I went round to the rear of the cottage and saw the place where the little 'privy' had been, where I had managed to secrete my life savings under the old wooden seat.

The cottage was being renovated and when I explained to the builders that it had been my home many years ago, they were only too pleased to let us go inside and look around. Once inside, no more proof was needed. Unbelievably, the built-in cupboard where my toys used to be kept was still there. Clem was having a field day with his camera, taking shots of everything. I knew that Clem had no further doubts in his mind, but I wanted to do one last thing so as to truly convince him, and again I took his hand. Leaving the property by the back gate, we took a further short walk and arrived at what used to be the school gate. It was exactly as I remembered, school railings and all.

"Clem," I whispered, "This is the nursery school I went to."

Clem whispered back, "Barbara, from the way you described it to me, I can tell it is. And I've a weird feeling of déjà vu."

I will never forget how I felt that day. I experienced a kind of release. In a way, it was a closure, putting the seal on all those yearnings to return to the place of my happy and innocent days, which had surfaced so often and could not be satisfied. I did have a few disturbing thoughts about the way I had been taken without any warning from a calm, loving home and literally pitched head first into the unwholesome world of a family of gypsies, from a soft feather mattress, to a bed of nails;

from a safe haven to a snake pit, and not yet five years old. Here had been mental cruelty at its worst and of course there were to be many more instances of abuse in my life from then on. I turned and took Clem's hand once more. It was time to leave the past behind.

Chapter 11   The Ghosts From My Past

In 1967 Dr. Christian Barnard carried out the first heart transplant in Capetown. Louis Washkansky, the recipient, lived for eighteen days. Elvis Presley married Priscilla; there was a disaster in space when the Soviet craft Soyuz crashed killing cosmonaut Komarov; Katherine Hepburn won an Oscar for best actress in Guess Who's Coming to Dinner? It was also the year when the poet laureate, John Masefield died, as did Sir Malcolm Sargent and Vivien Leigh, and Donald Campbell died on Coniston Water attempting a water speed record. Barbara Hall died in 1967 also. But this death was unique in that Barbara Hall had never existed.

Of course, I was Barbara Worrall in 1967, but until I was married I had been Barbara Hall, or so I thought. It was because of the constant niggling doubts in my mind that I went to obtain my birth certificate. There had always been secrets and mysteries in my life as far back as I could remember and the memory of some of those traumatic events of my childhood still intruded and had the power to unnerve me and to doubt myself.

This was not the first time I had discovered that I was not Barbara Hall. Shortly after my sixth child Amanda (Mandy) was born, I made two visits to the registry office in Shakespeare Street. On the first two occasions the registrar told me that I did not exist but the third time a birth certificate for Barbara Shaw was procured and then imposed upon me. I was not unfamiliar with the name of Shaw, as my half-sister Lily had that name. She had also used the name Hall, even registering her own firstborn in that name. This discrepancy of names was not discovered until December 1990. It has never been our intention to reveal these irregularities in order to upset someone else's past but, unless we do, how can we possibly expose those responsible for ruining my life and at the same time show that my circumstances were not just an isolated incident?.

Many of us will admit to keeping a skeleton in the cupboard, I suppose – something from the past that we prefer remains hidden. My cupboard is overflowing with skeletons – from my childhood and teenage years, through my working life and a sham of a marriage, to that unforgettable day in 1967 when I discovered that I was not the woman I thought I was. But unlike most, I would be happy to get my secrets out into the open – if I only knew what they were. One skeleton that continually rattled was the abuse I had been subjected to as a child, following my abduction by the people whom I knew as Robert and Violet Hall and who professed to be my parents. Violet was a bully and treated me harshly and Robert, although he could be a kind-hearted man, demonstrated his unfitness as a father by taking me into his bed. Even at a young age I knew that this was not the way that any true parents would treat their child.

Family life? I never felt part of a family and my early life was merely an existence. There were no words of love or encouragement and certainly no emotional security. And it didn't improve. Indeed, as I grew up, it became progressively worse until the day that I summoned the courage to put an end to Robert's antics. Violet did stop hitting me eventually, but the torrential verbal abuse continued until I left home.

I remembered being paraded in my Sunday best, especially when Henry Hall came to visit. These occasions were not unannounced; we always knew the day, the time and the venue. Sometimes he would visit us at the "Varda" wagon wherever it had come to rest. He always gave Violet money and had a lavish gift for me, but never anything for Lily. This was strange and caused a lot of jealousy between Lily and me but there was no need for her to be jealous, I never got to see it after he left.

How we came to be notified of his impending visits and by whom remains just another mystery; certainly there were public pay phones on our travels, but I never saw either Robert or Violet use any. I don't suppose Violet would have known how to. I don't know whether she could read, she certainly never picked up a newspaper. Robert did, he was fond of the racing page. His fondness for the horses was such that on one occasion when we were living at 589 Carlton Hill, Nottingham, he left taking all the rent money, so I cannot say much for his responsibility as husband and father.

Robert Hall, Henry Hall – was there a connection, or was the surname another strange coincidence? What happened to all those presents Henry Hall brought me? I don't suppose I'll ever know, but they were never seen again by me in the confines of the "Varda". Henry Hall would sit me on his knee, and say I was his favourite child. I do not ever remember him paying any attention to Lily and I sincerely do not mention this out of pettiness or to get my own back for the way she treated me all those years ago.

I would not want to hurt Lily in any way. There were times when she was very good to me. For instance she was the only one who would take me to the hospital when I had to have treatment for my smelly, runny ears. Violet never would, though it was she who regularly gave the same ears a battering when she lost her temper. It was Lily, at the age of eleven during an almighty bust up between Violet and Robert who said, "Come on, get your coat, we're off."

We literally ran away together and walked for miles and miles in the pouring rain until we noticed a house with a light on. Holding my hand, Lily took me up to the door and knocked. The door was opened by a woman who was aghast at our sodden appearance. Lily begged a drink of water as an excuse to ask for a night's shelter, saying we were lost and didn't know the way home. However, the woman didn't buy it and sent us on our way. I kept on crying and Lily was not very happy with me so we kept on walking until we came to another house. By this time it was really late, but she had more success here and we were offered shelter just for the night. How we got back to our parents again I couldn't say. Certain information remains locked away in the depths of my memory and is probably best left undisturbed.

Honest answers to these perplexing questions were the only way to lay the ghosts of my past and also those that would go ahead of me, waiting around each corner. My husband was indifferent to my plight and thought I was being silly and making an unnecessary fuss over the identity issue. One of my biggest worries was the fact that my marriage was not legal and my six children were therefore illegitimate. How do you continue with normal living, having that kind of anxiety weighing heavily on your shoulders?

Today nobody bats an eyelid at children being born out of wedlock, with different fathers or even no father at all, but in the so-called permissive sixties, it was not something to be proud of and although society then portrayed itself as having a liberal-minded anything goes attitude, the consequences of irresponsible behaviour were not that well tolerated – life was changing but attitudes were slow to catch up.

Chapter 12   Shocking Secrets

Anyone who has had to live with a secret that they feel is too personal and shameful to share with another human being, will know what a profound emotional and psychological effect it can have. It takes over your life and becomes an obsession and the more you try to escape from it, the more difficult it becomes to continue living a normal life. I had become used to living in an atmosphere of secrecy – Robert and Violet rejoiced in keeping things from me and a typical response to a simple question would be a blunt 'Mind your business', (often accompanied by a thick ear), or a blatant lie, which would turn out to be about as far from the truth as possible. However, I eventually became seasoned to their devious ways and, largely ignored them as much as possible, finding it easier to remain ignorant.

But when you discover something about yourself, something too awful, too shocking to reveal, it can bring you to the brink of despair and that is how I felt when I discovered that my birth had been falsely recorded. The feelings of isolation and loneliness nearly drove me insane. Who could I turn to? Who could I trust? This was an aspect of my life I just could not come to terms with. My childhood had been destroyed. It was a terrifying experience to be snatched from a happy life, taken from a loving family environment, to be plunged head first into one of isolation and deprivation; to a world where the only certainty was that I couldn't rely on anyone. Not even my parents. For most of us, childhood is a time when we feel most secure, when we learn to trust those around us, and we know the feeling of being loved. That is how it was for me during the time I spent in the cottage. I cannot find a reason or even an excuse that would satisfy any impartial mind as to why these people took me to their world, to their way of life when it was clear that I was not even wanted by them, let alone loved. I can never erase the nightmares; nothing will ever soothe the hurt of losing forever a most important part of my life.

Since meeting Clem I have poured out my soul to him; every fragment of my being, and he has put up a truly commendable fight to reveal the truth on my behalf. I am as sure as anyone could be that he will never let me down and I know that, as long as he breathes, he will continue with what has become a crusade to expose the lies and deceit as well as those responsible for this inhuman and unlawful cover-up.

The question that I constantly struggle with is, why me? What did I ever do that was so awful that I must accept a false name and, even worse, be forced to live out this falsehood for the rest of my life?

I was a frequent visitor to the Mecca bingo hall on St Ann's Well Road. After a tiring day of household duties, it was a welcome relief to get out of the house for a while. On most occasions I would be accompanied by one of my daughters or a friendly neighbour. Playing bingo helped to take my mind off the awful secret of my birth which I had only recently discovered and which filled me with fear and dread. I did not know what to do, or to whom I could turn and, however hard I tried, I could not push it to the back of my mind for long. It became rather like one of those irritating flies always buzzing around and impossible to swat away.

Naturally, tension began to build up and I was being given very searching looks at times, and hearing the odd remark such as, "You look ghastly", "Don't look so worried", "What's up with you?" etc. I learned to shrug it off, pretending that everything was fine. Those sessions at bingo seemed to bring a little normality back into my life and for a while, in the company of others, I could behave like a normal person with a normal life. Then, at the end of the evening, it was back to my secret world of despair again.

I prayed for a way to bring it all out in the open without letting my family down. I had no wish to bring disgrace on them; my own shame was already too much to bear. There was no easy way round it and in the weeks and months ahead; I seemed to operate on auto-pilot. After nights of tossing and turning in anguish, my days would begin at the crack of dawn, to be filled with the usual round of cleaning, cooking, laundry, lighting the fire, and so on. The house was always bright and cheery when they all got up to go to school or work. I never let them down.

Did they let me down? How can I answer that? They are my children after all, and nothing can change that fact, but could things have been different had they treated me with a little more understanding? It is only as we grow older that we build up emotional experience and learn how to deal with our feelings and those of the people close to us, so I cannot put any blame or shame upon them, but I hope with all my heart that, one day, they will understand how I felt and why I acted in the way that I did. I have only this to say to them now: Truly, I did not abandon you. At the time, I felt that it was the only thing I could do to save you from the destructive humiliation and shame that I had brought upon you all through my ignorance. But never forget, it was a contrived ignorance, forced upon me and carefully controlled by those who wished to keep to themselves the truth about my birth. Their raw materials were shocking events, thickly coated with shameful lies, leading inevitably to the shameful and shocking secrets I am only now able to disclose.

Chapter 13   More Questions Than Answers

Most of us have secrets and unexplained mysteries in our lives from time to time. They give us something to think about, to puzzle over and, sooner or later, we come up with an acceptable answer and move on, no longer preoccupied with whatever it was that troubled us. In my case, question after question after question has made my life one long unexplained mystery and my search for the answers continues. The irony is that asking one question invariably leads to another, which in turn prompts another and so on, and yet the answer to just one question would provide the means of answering all the others.

Who am I? Who were my natural parents? Why was I so cruelly taken from a loving home to live with a gypsy family that made my life a misery? Why did the famous bandleader Henry Hall visit me, bringing me lavish gifts and calling me his Lady Barbara? What was the connection between Henry and Robert Hall, why did a celebrated musician pay visits and large amounts of money to a family of travellers? Why did Robert Hall once inform me that I would never be able to draw a pension in that name. Clem was with me when this was said and, to this day I don't know whether he was referring to my name of Hall or, my married name of Worrall. When we tried to question further he pleaded senility and would not elaborate.

Why did I have to take a parent with me to post the Banns of my forthcoming marriage and what was said between Robert Hall and the registrar that was so secret they made me leave the room? Why was I told never to say anything or it would mean both of them being locked up for six months? Who was Robert Shaw? Why was Violet so cruel and unloving towards me? On the other hand, why was her sister Lily just the opposite – loving and kind and maternal. If these dark-eyed gypsies were my real parents, how come I was a blue-eyed blonde?

Why was the ID number given to me during the war so meaningless? How have I managed to end up with seven National Insurance numbers, none of which are recognized by the so-called authorities, and who do these numbers actually relate or belong to? Why was I denied a passport for more than eighty years and kept a virtual prisoner in this country, unable to travel abroad and see something of the world? Why have I, on numerous occasions, been denied medical treatment and found it almost impossible to obtain essential medication for my health problems? Why have I been arrested for bigamy when I was told that my first marriage was not legal?

All these questions have answers, if only we could gain access to the truth. The one which overrides them all and which has tormented me all my life is 'Who were my birth parents?' I want to know who I am, that's all. The majority of the population does not even have to think about this question, but there are times when I can think of nothing else. But probably equally important in my quest to find the truth is the question, Who registered my birth on 9th June 1923? My so-called father Robert Mark Hall, when challenged, claimed that it was my Aunt Lily who had dealt with the registration details and I also learned that when Robert and Violet discovered what she had done there was an almighty row. And that throws up yet another question - why was Lily registering my birth at all, if she was not my mother? What other reason or motive would she have had for doing so?

My earliest recollection of my Aunt Lily is when she used to visit her sister, my so-called mother. Now then, here hangs a big question mark over which sister was my biological mother. If I were Violet's daughter, why did she so frequently say, "Lily, are you taking her back with you this time when you go?" Sometimes the request would be put in a different way, "...and take that f***ing brat with you, out of my sight!" Often Lily would plead that she couldn't because of her profession, but always relented when she looked at me. I knew that she loved me. In fact, I longed to be with my auntie because she showed me love and care and genuine affection, something I never had or even dared hope for from Violet.

Several times whilst staying with Aunt Lily she would say, "Come on Barbara, let's take some lunch to X (one of her men friends who must have been a navvy, digging a trench a short distance from where she lived in Banbury). Then as an extra treat she would take me to see the statue of the lady on a white horse at Banbury Cross. Such memories of my Aunt Lily have never faded even though it has been over seventy years since those events took place. They are fond memories and I treasure them.

Aunt Lily was full of fun, rather a mischievous person, and there was quite a lot of rivalry between her and my so-called mother. On one occasion she said, "Come on Barbara, I will teach you a song - 'Here Comes the Galloping Major'. It wasn't difficult to learn and I used to make her laugh with my "Bumpety, bumpety, bumpety, bump, here comes the galloping Major, all the girls declare he's a millionaire, ay, ay clear the way, here comes the galloping Major".

When I returned home, more often than not I would have to suffer some gross indignity for having stayed with my aunt, like scrubbing the floor as a kind of penance, and of course if it were not to her liking, Violet would make me do it again and again, just out of spite. It was at just such a time that my mind drifted back to my fun-loving aunt and the song she had taught me and, as I could see no sign of my mother, I would burst into song "Here Comes the Galloping Major" when, Whack! At the side of my ear she hit me with the flat of her hand. I was too surprised even to cry – it felt like a fire alarm suddenly going off inside my head. I never saw her coming and wouldn't have started singing had I known she was anywhere near. She was livid, exuding undiluted hatred. She screamed, "Never sing that song in this household again, it's that trollop who's taught it you and you're a trollop just like her!" Why was Violet so hostile to her sister where I was concerned?

Nobody was ever in Violet's good books for long, but she did have her (rare) moments. When, at times, I had washed her feet for her, and cut her toenails, it seemed to ease away some of the pent-up rage that she was feeling. I know she didn't have a pleasant time when as a young child: she and her sister and brother were incarcerated in the workhouse, so I suppose the way she treated me was a reflection of her own childhood misery. Resentment and bitterness, tragically, had left her with no capacity to love. But she was adamant in her refusal to reveal the dark secret of my past and I can never forgive her for that. The question is why was she so vehement in denying me the truth? What was she so afraid of, the truth itself?

She often asked me to look in her hair for head lice. This sounds strange, but in a way I actually enjoyed searching through her head. At these times I felt wanted and close to her which was not very often. Then Dad would come in from work, and now I think about it, the first thing she would say to him was, "You know Bob, our Barbara's a good girl really, isn't she?" That seemed to be a signal, because I would then have to stay in for the evening, which invariably meant another round of sexual abuse. What kind of monster is a mother that can knowingly allow such atrocities to be carried out on her daughter?

Sometimes now, as I lie in my bed, I mull over the things that happened to me during my time with the Halls, trying to identify the missing link in this whole sorry saga. I pray constantly that I shall be able to settle this mystery whilst I still have a few years left to enjoy some semblance of normality. Surely I am entitled to that, and I ask nothing more than the answers to my questions. Then I can put my life in order and be free from the shackles of officialdom once and for all. For four decades, assisted by my rock, Clem, I have been searching for the answers to all these questions and many, many more besides.

One final question:

Do you really think I could have imagined all this?

Chapter 14   Wall Of Silence

Those in positions of authority who believe that they have the right to control people's lives have a most unskilled, but effective way of avoiding or fielding awkward questions. They simply duck the issue. Pass the buck. Put the CLOSED notice on the desk or on the door. Anything but deal with you in an open, direct way. However, these officials do seem to have the knack of somehow separating the mundane and harmless from the sensitive and possibly explosive issues. This is where they are at their most skilful and imaginative. They excel at conjuring up clever excuses, the ambiguous sort, which are impossible to argue with, and which they use to tell you the matter is closed.

With the introduction of the Freedom of Information Act on October 2nd 2000, I tried with the help of Clem to discover my wartime National Identity number, because after the war years it mysteriously vanished. If I ever asked my parents about it, they would shrug their shoulders unhelpfully and say I must have lost it after I left home in 1945 to get married.

I never realized how important that document was to me. It was supposed to continue with me through the rest of my life. It was to be used as a pivot for registration with the NHS and incorporated into the number displayed on one's medical card, but I don't remember ever having a medical card. And between 1967 whilst cohabiting with Clem, to the present day, I have somehow acquired five different NHS numbers. My life seems to me to be shrouded in so much secrecy and innuendo that it has slowly become a living hell. Only recently, someone described me as the Immaculate Conception!

My wartime ID number, which I was eventually successful in obtaining, is claimed to be RMCU74/4. The cost of acquiring this in real terms was one thousand eight hundred pounds, of which one thousand pounds is still owing to the firm of solicitors, Berryman Shacklock of Nottingham. This debt would have been settled had it not been for the Benefits Agency, who was on to the fact that we had renewed our attempts to establish my origins and lift the veil of secrecy obscuring my early years.

It seemed a good idea to go with what we were sure of; I was certain that during the war years I had a number and an identity card and was issued with a gas mask. After much prevarication by the Office of Populations Census and Surveys (OPCS), we received a response with my supposed identity number, but not before our solicitor had read them the riot act under articles 8 and 10 of the Convention of Human Rights. When she rang to say that she had received my ID number I was over the moon – at least I could now build on it to try and find out where everything had gone wrong.

Clem is very shrewd. He said in a very calm and precise manner, "Could you tell me what that number is?" There was a slight pause before she responded and read it out "RMCU74/4". Without hesitation Clem replied, "That is not her number." She was puzzled by his remark.

"Come on Mr. Clements, we have gone to a great deal of trouble over Barbara's war time identity number, it must be hers, what other reason could there be for not providing the right number?"

"Listen," said Clem, "I have made a study of how these numbers were issued, and I am confident I can prove to you that it is not her number. The last number rules out the possibility that it is Barbara's – yes, OK, I know it is only one number, but it does make all the difference."

At that point, we decided to leave it there for the time being, and discuss it further at our next appointment. Clem and I then headed back to the car. I knew he was deep in thought about the conversation we had just had and, at such times, I knew that it was no use trying to question him further. Not that I could think of any more questions, quite frankly.

Yet again, I felt somewhat beleaguered and deflated to be beaten on some lame duck excuse, all because someone must save face in a matter that didn't really concern them personally. This was the same old story of my life - getting nowhere fast. On hold. I wanted some answers now. In fact I felt so desperate, I wanted them yesterday.

We drove from Arnold to the Wilford Road area, and then turned into the car park of the Nottingham Archives Office. Clem was determined to discover who it was that lived at 239 St Ann's Well Road in 1939 when it was claimed to be me, and at the time when that National Identity number was issued to me. Now, if I am able to remember being abducted from a cottage in Hertfordshire at the age of nearly five and still able to trace that cottage some sixty-nine years later, then surely I should be credited with knowing that I never lived at 239 St Ann's Well Road when I was sixteen.

Someone, somewhere, somehow had got it all wrong. So very wrong. But this all smelt strongly of cover up. No matter which way we tried, we always encountered a brick wall. This quest for the correct information quickly became our every day task, and off we would go, with high hopes that this would be the day we would track down that vital piece of research, the last piece of the puzzle, but of course it never was. I knew of no other way to help Clem. It was no use pleading with him to give it up. He was a man on a mission and it was useless to even think such a thing let alone suggest it to him. Clem was his own person, and always said if you are going to start anything make certain you can finish it. If you want a good result and good standing, you have to give it everything you've got. I couldn't fault him.

He showed the same determination to succeed in every project he undertook, whether it was of a practical nature such as decorating, joinery, and DIY, or the more challenging 'bureaucrat-busting' at which he was now rapidly becoming an expert.

In the Archives Office, we readily found the section we wanted, and… bingo! There it was in black and white. Henry and Nellie Orme lived at 239 St Ann's Well Road according to the 1938/39 and 1939/40 electoral roll. As Clem said, we now had the ammunition, and all we needed was the cannon. Other people in the building must have thought us crazy; we were unable to conceal our exuberance, our glee, and I have to confess that I shed more than a few tears of joy. At long last we had, after a very long search, a piece of evidence which said 'here, look at your records once again, discover how you got it wrong at my expense and put it right.'

The days spent waiting for the next appointment with our solicitor seemed endless, but eventually the day was upon us, and off we went with renewed enthusiasm. We would give them a copy of our exciting discovery and see what action they would take, which should surely include further letters to the OPCS. This correspondence, together with our appointments, was costing one hundred and seventeen pounds an hour. It was a huge drain on our resources and, when the Benefits Agency suspended our income support, because I refused to provide them with the national insurance number ZW077670D (because I knew that it had never been issued to me), this put paid to any further legal assistance with this firm of solicitors.

Our solicitor was astounded at what we had discovered. She even remarked that her skills were too costly for us, that Clem was getting the results that she was being paid for, and this made her feel somewhat guilty. She also complimented Clem by saying that he probably knew more about certain aspects of the law than she did herself. However, she did agree to write to the OPCS again, stating that I never lived there and also the names of the actual occupants at the relevant time. But guess what! Another brick wall. A wall of silence met us yet again.

Chapter 15   Second Bigamous Marriage

The day was approaching and with each hour, I was becoming more and more nervous, particularly as our solicitor had told us we would be arrested if we insisted on going ahead with our plans. The day in question was 14th February 1992. St. Valentine's Day was the day Clem and I had chosen to marry for the second time. It was Leap Year and I had earlier proposed to Clem, who said he would be delighted to marry me, but gently asked whether I had considered the consequences? A dream honeymoon, followed by a life of wedded bliss? Not quite. It would mean almost certain arrest and the ordeal of facing more shameful publicity.

We were living in Birmingham at the time, at 19, Nineveh Avenue, Handsworth and Clem had his eye on a beautiful ring in a jeweller's shop nearby. After accepting my proposal of marriage, he said, "Come on; let's have a proper job this time. I've seen a smashing engagement ring in Roberts' closing down sale. It's a beauty and expensive but we can get it for less than half price!" He persuaded me to go with him to the shop and pointed it out to me in the window. It was a three-quarter diamond solitaire set in 18ct gold and absolutely sparkled with brilliance. It was exquisite and marked down from £1450 to just £650. We went inside and I tried the ring on, to find that it was a perfect fit. Clem paid a deposit on it. It seemed somehow that it might have been made especially for us. That ring came to mean such a lot to me and you can perhaps imagine how distraught I was when, some years later, we had to pawn it. We were desperate for money and had been refused any assistance by the state, so we had no option but to exchange it for some ready cash. We were given £250 cash for the ring and the pawnbroker wanted £285 to redeem it, but we could not afford anything like that at the time and so I had to let it go. I have had other rings since then, but none has ever meant as much to me as that one. It was extra special.

We returned to Nottingham at the beginning of February and after a few days Clem applied to the Registrar for a special licence to get married. I had already changed my name by deed poll from Barbara Hall to Barbara Goss. Some previous research into the circumstances of my birth together with various remembered details had compounded my belief that Lily, and not Violet, was my birth mother. I still had no idea who my father could have been, but at least I felt I had a more plausible identity by calling myself Goss. Clem's status of course was not a problem as he had been granted a decree absolute following his divorce and we actually managed to get through these preliminaries without any queries about my birth certificate.

The day we had both been waiting for dawned in a cloudy, moody sort of way, but thankfully brightened up later when the sun broke through. I was extremely nervous and Clem kept making little jokes in an effort to distract me. He is very good at doing this and he did manage to calm me a little. However, when we went to register for our planned forthcoming "Valentine's Day" marriage the Registrar appeared. My stomach just somersaulted and when he said he would be with us in a moment and we had to bear with him while he tapped away on a very old 'sit up and beg' typewriter, I really got cold feet and tried to leave. Clem, however, had other ideas and held on to me tightly, whispering that it would be all right. And it was all right; life was good again...for nearly five weeks after the ceremony. Now I had three marriage certificates, which seemed complicated to many others but, never to us, we were well in control of all our faculties. What we were doing was right and proper within the constraints of the law of the land. We had the nerve to do what we did, even though it appeared confrontational, when were we going to be permitted to put our cards on the table, why did every attempt turn out to be so unilateral? After our marriage on that Monday afternoon, after our second marriage in the space of nine months, we felt closer even more now, because our expectation was, it could be short lived. Who ever heard of anyone getting away with one bigamous marriage, let alone two. I have to say, although there was the dread of the knock on the door, I was deliriously happy, Nothing, not anything,could shake my resolve!

Friday the thirteenth. Clem called it 'Black Friday'. Yes, on 13th March, we were arrested by Birmingham CID officers and taken to Steelhouse Lane police station for questioning in connection with the alleged bigamy offence. I had the shock of my life when the policemen came to the house to arrest me. I had known all along of course, that this was a possibility but after the passage of a month, I became less anxious, falsely believing that this time our marriage had been recognized and accepted and we were at last going to be left alone to live our lives in peace, which is all we have ever wanted.

Clem, being legally divorced, was obviously not guilty of bigamy, but he was arrested for perjury, for which the maximum jail term was seven years. He was treated very shabbily and had no solicitor present. He was not even granted the obligatory phone call. Eventually, however, the enquiries were dropped. Well, how can you be charged if you have no legal identity? Also, how can you be prosecuted for marrying bigamously when your previous marriage was apparently not legal in the first place? I had been told that I could not obtain a divorce from George Worrall because I was not legally married to him. An annulment was not an option because this had to be applied for within three years of marriage, so what was I to do? This was Catch 22 in action.

A further complication arose from the fact that a second marriage, whilst still married to the same person, was not valid either.

But how could we be 'still married' if the first one was not valid to begin with? A couple are legally required to provide the correct information regarding marital status when first registering their intention to marry. As I do not even know what the 'correct information' is in my case It appears that we cannot satisfy the requirements and may never be able to legalise our relationship. It seems to be a case of damned if we do and damned if we don't!

We had arranged to have witnesses at the ready and they had been made fully aware that they could be committing perjury if we went through with this second marriage. However, we had come this far and if our getting wed was to turn out to be the crime of the century, well we were going all the way with it and to hell with the consequences! We didn't see what else we could do in the circumstances.

I was proudly displaying my engagement ring and the registrar commented that it looked expensive. Clem's reply was typical.

"I have decided to make an honest woman of her after a twenty-three year courtship and before I take her back to Ireland, the country of my origin."

It was then that the registrar made a surprising remark.

"I hope you don't mind me telling you but, you're illegitimate." Clem was taken aback by this comment and asked him to explain his remark. He replied that Clem's parents were married in Ireland and their marriage was not therefore recognised here in England. Clem asked how the situation could be rectified. He knew that he had been born in Dublin but he had always believed himself to be British. Was there no end to these dilemmas? The registrar said there was no way it could be rectified, as Clem's parents were no longer living.

How was it possible for him to be so well versed with our situation? He had certainly done all his homework. We then realised that what goes around comes around, as the old saying goes. The newspaper story some three months earlier announcing our intention to marry on Valentines Day had set off the tripwire and they were ready and waiting for us.

I had cold feet by now and tried to persuade Clem that we shouldn't go through with it. I reminded him again of the warning from our solicitor that it would mean immediate arrest. Did we really want more trouble? Was it time to call it a day? Clem would not be moved. His heart was set on it and his only comment, through gritted teeth was, "In for a penny, in for a pound. We are going ahead with this marriage and they can do what the hell they like!"

He had assumed his cavalier attitude and I remember thinking that he would be about as easy to shift as the Rock of Gibraltar. The ceremony did go ahead that day and we were again pronounced man and wife. However, it was not long before we were arrested by the police and held for questioning in connection with charges of bigamy and perjury. I was frightened out of my wits and I really was convinced that I would go to prison this time.

Shortly afterwards, however, we were told that no charges were to be brought against us, upon the recommendation of the Crown Prosecution Service. To say that I was relieved is an understatement, but Clem was outraged at the way we had been treated and said that if there were to be no charges, then what crime had we committed. He said it should go before a court of law if only to prove that we were now legally man and wife. But, of course, that was never an item on the bureaucrats' agenda.

Chapter 16   Passport to nowhere

I have been trying to obtain a passport for thirty years. My first application was to the Manchester office in the year 1976 and, was refused on the grounds that I could not prove my identity with my birth certificate. Since then, I have made countless attempts to get a passport, all of which have been unsuccessful. Consequently, I have been a prisoner in this country, denied the right to travel abroad and take holidays in the sun and see the world. All because of the false birth certificate given to me when I went to try to solve the mystery surrounding my birth, and which has tormented me ever since.

If a person was born before 1983, they are required to produce their birth certificate or adoption certificate in order to obtain a British passport. If their name has changed and, therefore does not match the birth certificate, then they must produce a document showing the date and reason for the change of name. Other acceptable documents are marriage and/or divorce certificates and, more latterly, civil partnership certificates. Moreover, if their name has changed more than once, they need to produce evidence of all changes of name; original documents must be produced and must prove that they are British by birth.

In my case, however, just trying to establish my true origin, let alone proving it, is like stumbling blindfolded through a maze backwards. As far as I have ever been aware, my parents (if indeed either of them were my parents, legally or otherwise) were Robert and Violet Hall. I believed this until I was forty-four years old when, after the many years of doubt and secrecy I encountered each time I tried to make sense of my childhood and upbringing, I decided that it was time to find out the truth that was constantly being denied me. That was when I went personally to the Nottingham Registry of Births Marriages and

Deaths in Shakespeare Street, and asked for a copy of my birth certificate.

Name?   Barbara Hall.
Date of birth?   20th May 1923.
Place of birth? 30 Cross Street, Nottingham England.

Sorry, there is no record of such a person. The response was devastating; not only the fact that I had just been told that I did not officially exist, but also that the situation was obviously even worse than I had imagined. I left that registry office with a very heavy heart and for many days I battled with my embittered emotions until the injustice of it all roused me once again to challenge the authoritarians whom I felt were denying me the basic right to know who I was, and the peace of mind and freedom that would at last be mine with that knowledge. The consequences of that second visit turned my whole world upside down. I was apparently not Barbara Hall, but Barbara Shaw, and the names of my parents were false. The nightmare had begun, and I have been battling ever since to find out the truth.

So with this kind of family history, how was it ever going to be possible to obtain a passport? How was Barbara Hall/Shaw/Goss/Worrall and later Barbara Clements/Jane Doe going to be able to prove her identity? Who would believe that this farce was taking place in twentieth and twenty-first century Britain?

Numerous solicitors have acted on my behalf, each one being intrigued by the background and tackling what they saw as an interesting challenge with great enthusiasm, only to find that some hurdles were insurmountable, whichever way they were tackled. Without exception, the jigsaw was always missing that vital piece which should have completed the picture. And of course that missing piece is my true identity, which still remains elusive.

There are various ways round the passport problem. The most obvious solution would be to change my name to Barbara Shaw. This would tally with my birth certificate and I could legally claim to be that person. But not truthfully, because I know that I am not Barbara Shaw and never was, because Robert Mark Shaw did not exist; there is no record of Robert Mark Shaw. Apart from the possibility of leaving myself open to prosecution, I will not perjure myself so as to conveniently let the Establishment off the hook and effectively allow them to brush the whole sordid mess under their carpet for the last time. That would be the easy way out – for them and for me, but as long as I breathe, I shall continue to strive to get at the truth – to lift the lid on this gigantic can of worms that wriggle relentlessly on, and on…

Another, more recent missive from the Passport Service decrees, that, a letter of confirmation from an older relative or responsible person such as a medical practitioner or minister of religion who has known me by all names would be acceptable as documentary evidence. Since no-one living has ever known me by all names, that idea is completely ridiculous and to me only serves to illustrate that the passport offices have not even grasped the point at issue. Or is it that they have chosen not to?

My hopes were raised again just a few months ago, when the Durham Passport Office agreed that they would accept a statutory declaration by me, exhibiting the various certificates in my possession and confirming my belief as to what really happened and why I changed my name. They went on to say that they only needed to be satisfied that I was born in this country to issue a passport. The solicitors dealing with it, in September 2005, were confident that this would conclude the matter to the satisfaction of all concerned and asked me to complete a fresh application for public funding so that they could proceed.

Eleven days later, the Legal Services Commission refused my application for public funding and, as I was not in a position to pay privately for legal costs, my solicitors were not willing to proceed further. However, a little more progress has since been made. In January 2006, I received a letter from UK Passport Service headquarters in London, which confirmed agreement that my entitlement to a British passport had already been established, subject to confirmation of identity. That seemingly, innocent word, identity. Again there is mention of the requirement of documentary evidence from an older relative but then they accede that 'due to your own advanced age a statutory declaration is probably more appropriate in this case.'

A letter dated 1st March to Welsh Assembly Member Ieuan Wyn Jones, who contacted UK Passport Service on my behalf, reiterated that a statutory declaration would be more appropriate to my circumstances, or indeed I could submit an affidavit already in my possession, covering all aspects relevant to my identity, (shouldn't that have been lack of identity?) Such a document 'might possibly be sufficient for the purpose'. The affidavit was sworn in June 1995 in an effort to try to obtain my retirement pension, which should have been payable to me from 1983. But that is another story, a further fiasco in this catalogue of denial of rights.

Having forwarded the said affidavit and, after thirty years of trying, I am now at last in possession of a passport, right? Wrong. My application has been refused yet again. The affidavit obviously was not 'sufficient for the purpose', and the whole sorry saga continues.

Chapter 17   Clem And His Roots

Just before Clem's 57th birthday in 1988, he discovered that he was one hundred per cent Irish. The authorities tried to deny him British citizenship stating that it was too late and claiming he had been brought into the country illegally. This harsh stance was mainly as a result of Margaret Thatcher's Immigration Bill of 1987. Just two weeks before his birthday Clem was notified by a high ranking official that he didn't have to represent him, implying that he was a free agent, and then said Clem was in the country illegally. Clem was angry at the arrogance of this person who professed to know more about him than he did himself. He left the office feeling dejected, miserable, and thoroughly ashamed to have ever called himself British.

It does seem reasonable to assume that in respect of something as important as your birthright, identity and nationality, it would be preferable, indeed advisable, for those with any information to impart such knowledge to whomever it relates to. Again we must return to the year of my own birth to enable me to tell Clem's story in full. About eight years before Clem and his identical twin brother John were born (on the 16th June 1931 at 152 Botanic Avenue Drumcondra, Dublin); their parents had eloped to the Irish Free State to get married, as the age of consent differed by three years to that of English law. Eighteen there, twenty-one here in England.

Philip George Clements wanted to marry Ethel May Gosling. Ethel apparently had her parents' approval, but Clem's father could not get the consent of his parents, even though his girl friend was at the time pregnant. There appeared to be no solution to this dilemma. Finally Mr. Clements asked to see the Personnel Officer at his work place, the world renowned John Player & Co.

After he had discussed his problem, it was decided that they would ship him with his wife-to-be and personal belongings to Ireland. His location was to be Dublin, where he would work as a machine operator and, in addition, teach the Irish workforce to become machine operators at the Dublin based factory.

When they both arrived in Dublin, they lived at separate addresses, so when they married on the 6th June 1924, Clem's father's place of residence was 30 Botanic Road, and his mother lived at 3 St Teresa's Place. A pre-condition of the move to Dublin was that they would have a new house built for them. The location was Botanic Avenue. The first time Clem and I visited Ireland was early in 1989, the first time ever that I had left the shores of Britain. It was also the first time I had been on a boat that I could remember, and we sailed by night, arriving early the next morning. Clem's only thought as we drove off the docks was to go to Botanic Avenue where he was born. Being unfamiliar with our surroundings, we had to ask for directions from several local people, who were most obliging. This was something we were not expecting, due to some of the tales we had been told about the Irish, but the stories were totally without substance. In our experience, they were warm, friendly and helpful.

When we approached Drumcondra, it was our intention to find the Parish Church of Glasnevin so, spotting a butcher's shop, we went and enquired there. Again, we were astounded by the help we received. When we asked the owner about the address where Clem was born and the Church where his parents had married, the butcher left his shop and his office (with thousands of Punts wide open to us and the rest of the world), saying he wouldn't be long and set off to make enquiries on our behalf. Clem said we had better go and stand outside in the doorway with all that money just lying there like that. It wasn't very long before a young Irish woman appeared and asked us why we were waiting outside. Clem explained that he felt uncomfortable with all that money lying around. We then discovered that the Irish were like that all the time; we learned that they never locked their doors when they went out, or even when they went to bed. I was fast falling in love with Ireland and its people and knew that I would take no persuading to go and live there for the rest of my days.

When the butcher returned he gave us some news about a Mrs. Mann who lived just round the corner from where we were, so we set off to locate her. The lady invited us in, and we discovered that her brother had strong connections with the Parish Church of Glasnevin. She then set about ringing her brother, and he arranged to meet us at the church, even though it was his wife's birthday. We waited outside the church for him and he led us inside and went to the safe where all the records of christenings, etc, were kept. Again, both the church and the safe were unlocked; we never saw him use any keys. The ledger was taken from the safe to disclose the family christenings and we learned that because of the death of Philip, (the third born), Gordon (the eldest brother) wasn't christened until after Joyce was born. Gordon and Joyce were both then christened on the same day.

We then examined the christening document for Clem and his twin brother, John. Later we went in search of Clem's birth address, 152 Botanic Avenue. The surprise here was that the property looked as if it had been built yesterday. It was situated in a row of terraced houses of white pebble-dash appearance, with small front gardens and their own entrance gates. Clem's first comment was that this couldn't be the place where he had been born in 1931. But nevertheless, and to my surprise, he walked up the path and without hesitation knocked on the door. I stood back a little, not quite sure what to expect, but I did venture forth when Clem beckoned as the door began to open. A tall, rather stately looking elderly lady stood there. Clem seemed a little embarrassed, but said in a clear concise voice, 'I am sorry to have disturbed you, but I was born in this house in 1931.' The door opened a little wider, and the lady hadn't yet spoken, when a very tall gentleman appeared beside her. He stood for a moment looking at us, then pointed an arthritic index finger at Clem, though not in an accusing manner. He said, 'You're George's son.' Clem said his father's name was Philip George, and the man finished his sentence with 'Clements - a chip off the old block, come on in!'

The old couple knowing that we had travelled overnight from England, wanted to provide us with a meal. We declined as we had already booked our accommodation on the west coast, and still faced quite a long journey before we arrived there. However, we stayed long enough to have a cup of tea and to learn how this gentleman came to know Clem's father. It turned out that he probably knew him better than anyone alive in Ireland, and it transpired that he had been trained as a machine operator at John Player and Co. in Dublin shortly after Clem's parents eloped there to get married. After we left, Clem realised he had not asked the gentleman for his surname, but said if he had to make a guess he would have said Walsh, because he remembered someone by that name who would send a goose before Christmas every year, and believed it could have been that person. He told us that Clem's father became very ill and this had caused him to pack up and travel back to England.

The rest of our holiday in Ireland was superb. The people were so friendly and kind, we were very reluctant to leave. We had planned another visit to the couple at the house where Clem was born, but the weather closed in and we had to cancel it. We encountered a very rough Irish Sea on our return passage to England. Our reason for travelling to Ireland initially had been to establish Clem's birth right to return to his native land. He had only recently discovered that he had lost all right to British citizenship, even though he had believed himself to be British through and through. Like me, he could not come to terms with this revelation and wouldn't even consider staying in England as a British subject. In fact he felt rather foolish that he had not known, and wondered how it was that these things could creep up on you un-awares and unannounced. Following this discovery about himself in 1988, we travelled to the Irish Embassy in October of that same year and were directed to the office of Eamonn Gildea, a high ranking official within the Embassy, who dispelled Clem's fears of being a stateless person. Had it not been for my own identity crisis, we could have established ourselves back in the Republic of Ireland many years ago. When I have that problem out of the way, we shall catch the first available boat to the land of many opportunities.

Chapter 18   The Year Of My Birth 1923

Chimes of Big Ben were broadcast by the BBC for the first time on the 31st December 1923. It is also claimed that I was born in that same year and would have been seven months old when the chimes were first heard over the air waves. What happened to me during the next four years is anyone's guess. I don't know, and if any other living person knows, they are not telling me. The truth was known at the time, and there are official records in existence today, but I have been told that these will remain closed until after my death. And what use will that be?

My so called mother once told me that I had been taken into hospital for emergency surgery when I was just ten days old. We have not been able to verify this even though we have exhausted every avenue of enquiry available, so it seems that this is another chapter in my life that I will not be permitted to delve into. My story itself is not important but there is another story behind it, which is, and when the missing pieces of this jig-saw are put into place, all the mystery surrounding the false registration and documentation of my birth will be revealed and out in the open. Then I may discover who Barbara Shaw was, and why she had to disappear.

No one should have to struggle for answers to the questions that they have a right to ask and, anyone finding themselves in similar circumstances to mine should be enabled to see that light at the end of the long, dark tunnel. The reason for concealment of the facts concerning my birth for over eight-decades has baffled the legal profession, genealogists and even government ministers. My case history has caused deep divisions, not only in my own family but also in disturbing ways with certain other people. Their attitudes towards me have been hostile and accusing, demanding that I should give up what they regard as my selfish fight to establish my own identity. All this just goes to show that they do not give a hoot for my feelings; why should they be bothered with it? Bury the past for their sakes. I cannot do that and will not and what I am desperately trying to prove is for my own sake and, will be my final goal. I have been deprived of a normal life for far too long. I want answers now while I still have a few years left and if that is considered selfish, so be it. Why should I not be able to have the enjoyment of lying in comfort on a warm, sunny beach somewhere? For most people, this is reality. Holidays in Spain, or Malta, wherever takes their fancy. For me, holidays like these have been just a dream, because of being denied a passport all of my adult life.

The most annoying aspect of my life is that it is full of innuendo. If whispers, nudges and winks could unlock the past, the puzzle would have been solved long ago. Each serious attempt to uncover any tangible detail from my dark past has been brushed aside as irrelevant and unimportant. What a story; what a life; what a huge hilarious joke! Well, I'm glad they have all had their fun and enjoyed a laugh at my expense, but it has only made me more determined to carry on with my fight for the truth and I still hope to prove the old saying, 'He who laughs last, laughs longest'.

Many, many times we have spoken with a registrar and invited her to put her remarks in writing. She has always declined. The matter did not conclude there and her signature later cropped up on a birth certificate, which enabled me to acquire a bigamous marriage to Clem. Other un-guarded moments have included such comments as, 'You don't have to know who you are. As long as we know, that's all that should concern you.' These people are just so unbelievable. I often wonder, does anyone really know the truth of who I am? Who are these grossly overpaid servants of our society, protectors of the faith (now that is laughable) and all that, who would put their jobs on the line in order to prevent me from uncovering the truth about my birth?

The day is approaching when this conundrum will have to go before the courts to find the answer to it. There doesn't appear to be any legislation in British law to enable me to put the past back in the cupboard so that I can get on with my life but one comforting thought, at least, is that I am not entirely alone in my isolation and alienation from normal society. Research has disclosed that there are another eighty thousand women in this country who, for whatever reasons, cannot obtain their rightful pensions and until landmark legislation is passed to set us free from the constraints of our supposed birth records, and we are permitted to challenge their authenticity, until this truth is established and I and others can prove who we are, we are all still adrift. As I was adrift, wandering with the travelling people all those years ago? Did I become an orphan of the storm? Despite all our efforts, I am still the Woman Who Never Was.

I suppose it is only fair to say that I do now receive a pension. But why did it take so long? It commenced one month before my seventy-ninth birthday. Some birthday greeting; I would only be eligible to draw a state retirement pension if I were prepared to accept pre-conditions. The conditions imposed upon me were that I would agree that I was still married to my husband George, and that I would draw my pension in my married name of Worrall, irrespective of my two bigamous marriages to Clem. One other clause stated that I had to accept this pension on National Insurance number ZW 07 76 70 D. No mention was made of the four thousand four hundred pounds we were deprived of, in an effort to persuade me to accept these conditions.

I have declared on numerous occasions that there is no way the aforementioned number could be mine. This amounts to gross maladministration; a direct dereliction of duty or, more intriguingly, a further attempt to conceal my true identity and origins. When these two giros arrived in the princely sum of seven hundred and nineteen pounds, and a promise that if I accepted, there would be compensation, and a further promise that if we obtained additional evidence my case would be looked at again, Clem strongly advised me not to accept. He said that it was a mere fraction of what I should be entitled to; throw it back and politely tell them to get knotted. I regret that I didn't take his sound advice because his words have come back to haunt me.

We now have that evidence which would blow my case wide open. At the time when that NI number ZW 07 76 70 D was issued - on the 24th September 1956 to Barbara Goss, I was then eleven years into my marriage as Mrs. Barbara Worrall. I also had a child barely ten months old and was two hundred miles away from the place of issue. How many more times do I have to state this is not my number? Neither do I believe (as suggested by an Ashfield Councillor), that it is duplication. No! I do not, and neither are the other six National Insurance numbers allocated to me since 1985. This is really not my problem and unless it is sorted out, we shall get nowhere. In which case, we stay with it until a satisfactory conclusion is reached. There are a great many women counting on my case going to the courts in order that they also can sort out their pension entitlements. We will try not to fail you.

As I write this chapter, the New Year is fast approaching. Will 2007 hold any new hope for me? I don't think so, more uncertainty seems most likely. Another bumpy road that leads me nowhere; a promise of a nice holiday, but I think that is a dream. Without the funding to finance such a journey I don't think it will happen. Are there any persons who would trade places with me? I very much doubt it. This illustrates how uncertain my life has become. The answers are out there, somewhere, but without the necessary legal assistance, will it ever happen? Not in my lifetime; for one thing I am denied legal aid and for another, my case is Statute Barred.

Chapter 19   A Lonely Childhood

As a child, I did not spend a lot of time actually on my own. Indeed, at times, there was more company around me than I needed or wanted. My loneliness was that bleak kind of isolation that comes from the knowledge that you are not really wanted, that you don't belong, or fit in. This creeping emptiness began on the day I was taken away from my happy little world in a Hertfordshire cottage, when living suddenly became merely surviving and everything I experienced from then on was alien to me and very frightening for a five-year-old.

Robert was not unkind to me in the way that Violet and my half-sister Lily were, but of course he had his own perverted reasons for that. I did make friends with other children during the times when we actually attended school but, again, Lily with her mother's jealous nature would always ensure that these friendships were short-lived. When I was taken from my safe little world at the cottage I was too young to understand why I was being whisked away to this roller coaster of a new life. In a matter of hours, in spite of my tender years, I started to become a different child. I was dramatically changing from a child who had been cared for, into a child that had to care for herself. This life was not suited to me and, somehow I sensed that this family was strange. Their world was peculiar and alien to me but there was no running away from them, had the thought even remotely entered my head. When I think back to those first hours, I live again the opening episode of what was to become a dreadful life. I have never been able to erase the memory of that day. No one spoke to me or I to them. I dared not and, anyway what could I have said even if I had been permitted to do so? Maybe that's how it was planned, to enable me to get used to my new surroundings. I know that I would have demonstrated my dislike for them all and I would also have asked to be taken back to the cottage and the couple I loved. They were so dear to me and I missed them so much.

It is sad that I never was able to contact them again from that day. I was lost to them and they were lost to me. This was a void in my life that was hard to reconcile. I convinced myself that I would one day return but my hopes slowly faded over the years although my memories never did. One day I hope I shall be lucky enough to learn more about that fateful day. There is a lot more information to be discovered and my dream is to fit together every piece of the puzzle that has progressively become more difficult to solve as the years have passed. I did manage to find my way back to that very cottage with Clem's help, and because of an article in the Hitchin Comet, I was able to make contact with Roy Jarman who lived in those cottages until nineteen thirty-two and, who stated in writing he was told frequently by his mother about the unfortunate child who was taken from the cottage nearest to the village shop. With this vital evidence supporting my claim, surely someone in high office could, and should now be able to help me cross that final bridge so that I can at long last put my life in order.

The thought is nice although the execution of it may not be. I cannot perceive anyone relenting to the ranting of a woman without concrete evidence and I know full well that it will yet again be passed off as pure fantasy and hearsay as it has been so many times before. Even my contrived birth certificate details have been described as a convenience to spare my mother's blushes. I regularly take a trip down memory lane, looking over my shoulder to the day I was taken from the cottage. It was an exciting moment for me when I found the old place again, but the chilling memories it stirred up were not so pleasant. Far from it. For a little girl of nearly five, it was a nightmare experience. I have also reached the conclusion that the whole episode had been well planned. It was not a spur of the moment decision and

111

I firmly believe the Halls knew in advance what day they were going to fetch me. I should have been in the nursery school in the village of Willian. I so enjoyed my days in that village and on waking in the mornings I used to prepare myself for school, under the watchful eye of the lady I thought of as my mother. I had been taught that cleanliness was next to godliness. 'Wash behind your ears' would be a friendly shout and, 'don't forget your neck, we can't have you going to school with a tidemark.'

All these things were a reassuring part of normal family life, to which I once belonged. It was an ideal place to be brought up in. Why? I never stop asking myself, why did it all suddenly have to end whilst I was so young? If I were ever asked what the cruellest thing I could remember happening to me, I would reply spontaneously, the day when I was taken away. For me it was the beginning of forty-four years of deceit and shame. How many hours we travelled with my new found family I'll never know. Nor will I ever know in which direction we went or to where. What I am sure about is that I cried for the whole journey. Looking up through the "Varda" wagon's molliecroft where I had been bundled, I saw daylight turn to dusk. I never moved and had nothing to eat or drink. No one enquired how I was or if I wanted anything, and that's how life was for me from that day until my marriage in 1945.

It was very late and dark when we pulled into a field somewhere. I became aware that there were others in the field, when I was told to climb out of the "Varda". Violet whispered through clenched teeth to 'keep away from those gypsies they'll skin you alive for a tanner.' Then we were told to get to bed. There was still no food, and this was to be the first time of not sleeping on my own. Sharing a bed with Lily was an experience in itself. I slept in the summer frock that I was wearing when I left the cottage, and the toy I had brought with me I never saw again. All I had in the world were the clothes I stood up in. I desperately wanted my mother; to be back with her again at the cottage and to see her loving face. I saw it in my mind and, heard her gentle voice bidding me goodnight, and my tears of anguish were uncontrollable.

This sudden switch in parents had a devastating effect on my whole life, which even to the present day, I cannot come to terms with. My inexorable search for answers and, the truth will continue, irrespective of the consequences. There has been much unhelpful innuendo from certain officials who, I am sure, could provide answers and possibly know far more than they are prepared to reveal. These are the people who remark, '...are you sure you want to know? You might not like what you discover; you're not prepared.' How would they know whether I'm prepared or not? It's my life and, all I have ever wanted is to be told the truth, the whole truth and, nothing but the truth and that's final.

Often, in an attempt to dissuade me, they would even try to intimate that Clem and I were brother and sister. This of course is beneath contempt, but so cruel it has to be mentioned, to demonstrate the extremes these officials were prepared to go to in order to block my human rights. Why I have been prevented from knowing my origins and biological parentage is beyond my comprehension.

Attempts to tell my story are met with incredulity. I tell it how it was, and how it still is, to some extent. Some people say they have never heard anything so crazy, and in these modern times of human rights and freedom of information, I am surely entitled to some answers. The problem is I have not yet arrived in their modern times; my time is still locked away and I am being denied the key. When I get my hands on that key, I will be able to open my Pandora's Box. A lonely child will surely be first to escape from the box, followed by the many evils that have blighted her life ever since. But the spirit of hope will remain; I have expectations and will never give up on my promise to myself – to make things right for the sake of that frightened little girl.

Chapter 20   Violet, Lily and Billy

Violet, her sister Lily and brother Billy were well known characters that frequented the Narrow Marsh pubs. Whenever there was any mention of the places that Violet frequented, foreboding words would burst from her lips, 'Don't ever let me catch you near the Broad Marsh or anywhere in that vicinity!' and we knew that she meant it. This was not an unusual warning; many parents demanded that their children kept well away from that area. When I used to visit Clem's house I heard it said to his brother and sisters and, later, I wondered if Violet's concerns were only because it was a notoriously evil place, or was she was worried that I might stumble across something that would arouse suspicion of who we were and what we were about. It also reminds me of when she used to say, 'If you ever see me out, never call me Mam in the street, and always call me Violet.' This would surely be considered a very strange request from a mother to her biological daughter, but I knew if I challenged it there would be no answers, other than a thick ear, maybe. The more I think about it, this was never related for Lily's ears, but only mine. Even Lily was reluctant to talk about what it all meant so, you see, you just had to let it go; Violet could be such a tyrant. To me now, it seems quite obvious that there were people she knew that were aware she had a daughter Lily, but were not intended to know that I was also a member of her family.

Even though there were stark warnings from Clem's parents to him and his siblings relating to the Marshes, this didn't deter Clem. He paid no heed as he was fond of a game of table tennis and snooker in these halls situated in the Broad Marsh. Narrow Marsh, which was in close proximity to the Broad Marsh, was notorious for its squalor and all kinds of criminal activity. It was eventually demolished in 1929 and had its name changed. It is now known as Cliff Road and has rows of respectable council houses built on it, but in former days it was a well known haunt for everything imaginable from thieving and brawling to primitive abortions. A favourite stunt of thieves would be to steal the clothes from the washing lines along with the clothes props and return later to sell them back where they had taken them from. No one dared challenge these bands of felons as they were so well organized. Eventually, those who had their belongings stolen learned the hard way, and secured them away until the next wash day.

Other favourite haunts visited by Violet and her brother and sister were the Corner Pin and the Old Dog and Partridge on Parliament Street. Lily used to entertain the punters by whistling popular tunes of the time and Billy would yodel. Billy had a glass eye and was well known to the locals. Lily was very beautiful and turned men's heads. Violet was jealous of her good looks as well as her popularity and would stir up trouble, calling Lily a trollop. It is true that Lily was a fully paid up member of the oldest profession and, because of her classy looks and accommodating manner, she attracted rich and influential men. I remember that Violet would frequently tell Lily it was time she took me back with her, as if she was my mother. Lily did have me to stay with her sometimes and I liked being with her but she was unable to have me very often, due to the demands of her gentlemen clients. Lily died in the sixties apparently of cancer and suffering great pain. To my sorrow, I still have not been able to trace her final resting place. After her death, it was discovered that Lily had adopted a little girl, Cathy, but she had been taken away from her, presumably because of her unsuitable 'career'.

William Goss and his wife Mary lived in constant turmoil and it was claimed that, in a frenzied attack, William (Billy) Goss beat Mary his wife so often that, this resulted in her death and poor young Billy and his sister finished in a home not unlike the workhouse. Violet, Lily and Billy were all very young at the time and it was alleged that their father William Goss (senior) himself had them institutionalized in the Cottage Homes (or workhouse) about the year 1910, because he could not cope with them after the death of his wife. I have no facts to substantiate any of this. One would presume that if he killed his wife he would have been locked up himself, either in prison or an asylum. We will continue to search for these records and hopefully we will find another piece to slot into this intriguing story.

These accounts of their incarceration were well talked of during family get togethers. My so called mother Violet would talk quite freely when she was in one of her better moods, such as the times when she asked me to do her feet. I would have to prepare a bowl of hot water and then I would soothe and wash her feet for her, and dry them before giving her a pedicure (and sometimes, while I was at it, a manicure.) Strangely, she would not let anyone else near her feet and afterwards, if I was careful not to upset her, I could be in her good book for days on end. There was a strange kind of closeness between us at those times which, sadly, never lasted long enough to mean anything. It was certainly a learning curve, surviving in this most wayward and unholy of households.

Violet would tell me of her time in the workhouse and, from her accounts of her incarceration; we can determine that conditions were very harsh indeed and Draconian by today's standards. She would relate how they were beaten with large wooden spoons, and then suddenly she would clam up as if the memory was more than she could bear. Her life was certainly not as it should have been and I don't believe that she or her brother and sister ever came to terms with the loss of their mother at their tender ages. Their plight would have been cruelly ignored and apart from having each other, there would have been no one to counsel or comfort them. Is my life a reflection of the way they were treated during their confinement? I regret being so critical of her now that I have come to understand more of what they must have suffered, and I would like to be able to say sorry but it is too late; they are long dead, forcing me now to seek answers elsewhere. When they were still alive I would have liked to have sat with them and talked through the events of my life, and this tragic, yet ridiculous situation I find myself in, and if I seem to be repeating myself, please bear with me; I have to grin and bear it. I am fully aware that I am asking the same questions more than once, and if this is boring, forgive me – isn't life a subliminal kind of an ass?

It was also a great wish of mine to sit with my own offspring in a quiet consoling atmosphere and try to explain the discrepancies and irregularities and events since I became aware of the fact that I was not who I was supposed to be. If only someone had been there to explain it all, but no one was there for me. Why, then, is it demanded of me to heal their wounds when I didn't have a soul in the world to help me? As I saw it, everyone was too busy getting on with their own lives to be concerned with me, after all I was only their mother, so what of any importance could there possibly be to bother about? These words may come as a great shock to some. 'Those are not the words from her mouth; way out of character,' they may say, but sadly this is the ultimate stance I have come to. It is what my lifelong struggle has brought me to and there can be no turning back now. These skeletons are not going back in the cupboard until they have been severely dealt with. They must be silenced forever for the sake of generations to come.

So here we are now just a few hours into the New Year, and Clem and I have decided to intensify our efforts. The best form of defence, we are told, is attack. We will decide the rules of engagement and, with nothing to lose, we will start to collate everything we have so far. We have to put it all into some semblance of order to compile a pedigree of all my family and ancestral connections. This could possibly reveal what it was that went so drastically wrong and may explain how my problem started.

We now know for sure that of the three of them – Violet, Lily and Billy, Violet was older than Lily by some four years. There is so far no evidence to substantiate Billy's age, but we do believe him to have been the youngest and, in those circumstances, probably also the most vulnerable at that time.

Chapter 21   Someone Else's Identity

Another unsolved mystery is the question of whose identity I was given when I was issued with my ID card during the war. Everyone residing in Britain before the onset of World War II had to be issued individually with an identity number, gas mask, and ration book, corresponding to an address. At the time of issue and allocation my age would have been sixteen years and four months. I was living with my parents Robert Mark and Violet Hall and, as far as I can remember, our address was either Rose Street or Manning Terrace in the St Ann's area of Nottingham. My sister Lily was two and a half years older than I but she had left the household some time previously, when our place of residence had been in Salisbury Street, Beeston. She had stayed behind as she wanted to be with her boyfriend Gerald, another reason she stayed behind was because she was pregnant, but somehow the dates don't add-up. I know I was twelve years of age at this time, my half-sister Lily was two and a half years older, I will do further research into our respective ages and, the area we were living at the time of this episode in my life.

This was a rapidly changing period of my life and some events are still something of a jumble to me; dates and places have become somewhat mixed up in my mind and it is sometimes difficult to differentiate between one place and another. However, the one thing I am absolutely certain of is that I was not living at 239, St Ann's Well Road at the time of the issue of my credentials. For the benefit of those who are unfamiliar with the numbering system, my ID number, RMCU74/4, comes out like this: RMCU was the designated area that the enumerator would visit, seventy-four would be the number of households compiling his register, and the four would put you in line of seniority. Clem's ID, RMDD208/6 is a similar area to mine, the enumerator had two hundred and eight households to compile and he was sixth in line in the family at the time of issue. This was clearly defined on his ID card. Head of the household and present in the house at the time the enumerator visited was his father, who would have been issued with number 1. His mother came next 2, then his elder sister Eileen 3, followed by his brother Gordon 4, second sister Joyce 5, then Clem, the first born of identical twins, 6, John, his twin, 7 and lastly, Derek, the youngest, 8. Clem actually still remembers to this day all the numbers he was issued with, even his Army number and his first PSV badge number EE30,731. But how is it possible that I had been stated to be the fourth in our household at that time when in fact I was next in seniority to my father and mother?

Then there are the National Insurance numbers and National Health numbers which have been issued to me at various times and in different places. The vast majority of the population, I believe, holds one National Insurance number and one National Health number throughout their lifetime. So why have I been given so many different numbers, and who do they actually relate to? I have tried to find out, but no-one has yet been able to give me an acceptable explanation.

Shortly after the onset of World War II everyone in this country was issued with a National Identity number and identity card bearing that number as proof of who you were. All kinds of people could challenge you to produce the document to identify yourself but it contained no photograph and, as far as I am aware, no further details other than name and address. Some of those who challenged me only did so for a bit of mischief, especially when my workmates and I entered the munitions factory where we regularly worked nights. These were happy times for me. I had a purpose in life. Occasionally, by prior arrangement, we would all meet up in the Foresters Arms public house before boarding the train to work the long hours in the bomb filling factory which was not only a dangerous job but also, hazardous, because of the chemical factor. All of us who were engaged in this work had to lather ourselves with thick cream to protect all exposed skin. We looked really weird, just like ghosts, with our faces and arms smothered in this white lardy stuff, but it was always good for a laugh. Laughter was something which had not really featured a lot in my life until then and I was now just beginning to emerge from my shell and starting to enjoy myself and I really looked forward to each working day away from the confines of the oppressive atmosphere of what was known to me as home.

When would it all end? It was surely too good to be true. I had never been allowed any freedom and my working life was a totally new experience to me. What had been forced onto me previously was now a million miles away. I could now live a little, make up for lost time, start to repair the damage done to me when I had suffered abuse of the worst kind, the unbearable isolation and alienation that I had endured day after day after interminable day. I have to ask myself, how did I survive it all? Clearly, I had been an unwanted child, but the question is, whose child? Will I ever know the answer to this burning question?

I seem to remember more of the events which occurred during those years than those of when I was quite young. Probably it could have been that now was the time when I could reflect on my life and what it had come to be. Also, I was no longer willing to be brainwashed into blind acceptance of what I knew to be unwholesome as well as untrue. I feel that in some way I knew that my assumed parents had lied to me constantly throughout my life. I had truly come out of the shadows, and was ready to challenge my oppressors, albeit with a somewhat subdued approach. I knew that Violet was a better master of the art of deception than I could ever be, or even hope or dare venture to be.

At this time I was still a welcome visitor to Clem's parents' house. They lived at 76 St Bartholomew's Road (also known as Donkey Hill), which was notoriously the steepest hill in Nottingham. Clem's house was just a few doors past Blue Bell Hill Road. Those were memorable days for me; I had an interest in these people whom I can speak of as friends of the genuine kind. There was always a buzz of activity especially with the younger ones, and I spent many happy hours with them, often staying over for days on end.

Sadly, another event turned this family against me after they saw my supposed father begging on crutches in the Market Place at Matlock, Derbyshire. From then on they were ashamed of me, and felt that I had deceived them. They were unprepared for the discovery that I had a father who could behave in such a mean and despicable way and decided that they no longer wanted to associate with me. And who could blame them? So the friendship that I had so cherished came to an abrupt and unpleasant end and once more I became the outcast; the pariah it seemed I would always be, cut off yet again from a normal life and normal relationships.

Clem's parents were stallholders in Matlock at the time they discovered my father begging, and what upset them more than anything was the fact that they knew Robert was not a cripple, and they also knew he was not a veteran of the Great War and his presence there was a masquerade and a deception that they would have nothing to do with. Again, because of his outrageous actions, I was on my lonesome yet again; not a friend in the world, as alienated and isolated as ever.

Is it any wonder that I grew up with a severe inferiority complex, unable to describe my worst fears, born innocent as we all are, but absorbing the wickedness of those around me and having to suffer the indignation and shame of it all to my dying day? What a cruel hand life dealt me.

In fairness to Robert, I should mention that he had at one time been injured in a Welsh mining accident and there had once been a reason for the use of crutches, so probably life hadn't dealt him a good hand either, but even if there had been an attempt to explain, would anyone have listened? And it does not excuse his cynical exploitation of a previous misfortune. No contact was made again between Clements family and myself and our paths never crossed until one day I was in the old market square in Nottingham heading towards the Council House, when I was spotted by Clem's sister Eileen. She had been my best friend all those years ago. I had never forgotten the shameful reason for the rift between us and I was therefore in haste to pass on by without being noticed. I was too late; she had already seen me and, to my surprise, called out my name with a friendly greeting. We chatted for quite some time. Clem was with her. At that time, I knew him by his first name of Cyril. I had two of my daughters with me, one of whom was still in a pushchair. Clem, I discovered, had become a smart and handsome young man of sixteen.

When we parted that day, it was to be exactly twenty years to the day when I walked into Clem's life. The first forty years were not all unkind to me but they failed to satisfy my need to find the explanations I was entitled to and so badly wanted. I felt I had been cheated out of my true title and inheritance and, more meaningfully, the truth about my ancestry. I was lucky in that I had a good husband who once worshipped the ground I walked on, and who took care of me. But for me that was not enough, there were issues that I needed to resolve and George was not interested. He simply never understood my situation, and who can really blame him for that? These last forty years have more than compensated and I wouldn't change a moment in spite of all the difficulties Clem and I have had to endure. However, I still want the answers to my questions. I will never relent until I know who I truly am.

Chapter 22   Battle For Identity

I know that there are others who, like me, do not have proper means of identity. Each of our circumstances are different, but we all share the same basic need – to establish our identities, to prove to the world that we do have a rightful place in it and of course, it is also a basic human right. Since I met up again with Clem in 1967 and told him of the mystery surrounding my birth and how it had affected me, we have battled constantly to try to uncover the truth. It has become an obsession now and until we get satisfactory answers to the many questions raised, we shall go on relentlessly pursuing the truth.

For me, proving my identity has become an almost impossible battle to win. There have been obstacles at every turn. I seem to clear one hurdle, only to meet another, yet higher one, and then a five barred gate. It has been an uphill slog all the way, but at last I suppose I am a little nearer to the truth and once it is all consolidated, we can then challenge officialdom through the courts. My life story contains many mysteries and one day all these secrets must be revealed. After all, we are now in the twenty-first century, not the dark ages, although I do not always find it easy to spot the difference. The bureaucrats continue to paper over the cracks as they always have.

In 1964 we received a letter from our solicitor confirming that she was disturbed by my case. We had previously presented to her eleven documents. These included my alleged birth certificate, marriage certificate and other documents concerning family members. Her reply conveyed to us that she was stunned and baffled by the evidence before her and we were greatly encouraged by her remarks that we should now be able to get a result. All the hard work would at last produce a satisfactory conclusion. But alas, no. It turned out to be another broken dream. This firm of solicitors seemed to be, at the time, determined enough to take on the authorities and tackle the problems relating to my state pension rights. They informed me that the priority would be to establish my right to claim a state pension. When this had been achieved and arrangements put in place for me to draw my pension, I should be able to live a normal life. Never having experienced such a luxury, I could make no comment, only wait in anticipation. The thought of soon becoming a normal person was very appealing; I could live with the idea of that.

As usual, it was not long before it all began to go wrong again. Our legal adviser belonged to one of the top firms of solicitors in Nottingham. Their practice was located in a grand listed building in Stamford Street. We were notified that she was no longer going to act on my behalf and another solicitor would be representing my case. Unfortunately, we did not get along with the new person. She suggested a compromise, but this was not an option. In spite of this, however, we did stay with the firm until we had a legal document drawn up appointing Clem as my Enduring Power of Attorney.

What was on offer and, we have nothing in writing to substantiate this, was that if we were prepared to accept any genetic fingerprinting linking Violet and myself, all costs would be met. What the solicitor did not know was that Clem had already thoroughly researched this possibility and found the outcome to be unsatisfactory. He wasn't trying to be obstructive or unreasonable but having contacted persons at the pioneering stage of this technique, he knew that this suggestion was improper and the so-called golden opportunity to put my life in order was deeply flawed.

It appeared on the face of it, that certain individuals were bending over backwards to help me. In fact all they were doing was simply painting another picture on top of the existing one. No one was prepared to strip the problems down to their roots and investigate the circumstances of what masquerade as my birth records. Officially Barbara Shaw is missing, so how is it possible that I could return after an absence of forty-two years? There was no paper trail, no hospital records, in fact nothing identifying Barbara Shaw with Barbara Hall.

If we are the same person, why have I never been permitted to know the truth about the matter? When I reached the age of consent and what was laughingly referred to as 'freedom', my parents should have come clean and explained the situation to me. They did not. Am I at fault for not insisting that the facts be made clear? How could I, when at that stage in my life I knew absolutely nothing of the irregularities concerning my parentage? For goodness sake, I was kept in the dark about it until I was forty-four years old and I am still in the dark today. Can anyone tell me how, without a paper trail and with my true birth records safely under legislative lock and key, I can identify whether I am Barbara Hall or Barbara Shaw?

This was the problem when applying for my state pension. Not just a nightmare for me, but also for the Pension Service, who repeatedly requested me to complete their many questionnaires. But if they didn't know, how was I supposed to know? You must tell us where you were baptized. Knowing my mother, this would have been by dedication with the Salvation Army. I never belonged to the Salvation Army, but probably for some obscure reasons of tradition, I had my own children dedicated through them as well.

Henry Robert Hall, the acclaimed bandleader and international entertainer who visited frequently, was also involved with the Salvation Army as a trumpeter. A certain writer on the Isle of Wight has rubbished my claims that he was ever involved with the family. However, Carol was not aware that over a considerable length of time we had thoroughly researched his connections, proving beyond doubt that he had strong ties with Robert and Violet. My half sister also played an accordion in a troupe called the Toreadors. She wore the Salvation Army uniform and regalia when she went on parades in the Beeston area of Nottingham. I used to go to watch, and I was so proud of her. My supposed father Robert taught her to play the accordion, and he was also very good on the concertina (squeeze box) and mouth organ, and, like Henry Hall, he definitely had an aptitude for music. The only thing he taught me was the Welsh National Anthem.

In later years whilst I was working on munitions at Luxfers bomb filling factory I was invited to an audition by ENSA who entertained the troops here and abroad. Without my knowledge, the girls at the factory had nominated me as I was often called upon to sing the popular songs during the war years. I was told I had a good singing voice and I have to admit I enjoyed singing; I had an ear for music then but sadly not so these days with the onset of deafness. Clem also loved a sing along during our earlier years together.

The day of my audition came. I chose the song I would sing and got up on the stage. Every one waited in anticipation and then I was overcome by stage fright and just froze. The accompaniment started into the song for the second time, but not a note came forth and I ran off the stage in shame and embarrassment and cried myself silly. But I do believe there is a strong connection with the Halls on Robert's side.

This complicates my life even further and again there is the question, why am I not permitted to know more? Why are there no tangible clues as to why this has dragged on for too many years? Probably if I hadn't flunked it at my audition, I wouldn't be where I am today. I am sure that if the audition had been a success, I would have had to travel abroad. Wouldn't I have needed a passport and would I have been refused one then, as I have until recently, because of the mystery surrounding my birth? Can someone please tell me?

Chapter 23 Tears Of Joy Or Tears Of Sadness

After many years of campaigning for an official identity and passport, it seems it has finally arrived, addressed to Ms J Doe. I have reservations about opening the envelope and feel anxious in case I am to discover that the passport contained within will be made out for someone else, or that it could be in one of my former names of Hall, Worrall, Goss or even Clements. I wouldn't mind the latter. After all, I have been through two bigamous marriage ceremonies to acquire that name. According to a remark made by a Nottingham solicitor, my two bigamous marriages to Clem, my common law husband of almost thirty-nine years, were more legal than my first marriage to George Worrall on 5th May 1945 at the Bristol Register office.

This passport in my legally adopted name of Jane Doe will open up a whole new world for me. I will now have recognition for all manner of things legal, social and official. After a determined and relentless fight with many prominent persons assisting me, could it be that after eight decades of life in the shadowy unknown, I have finally arrived at my goal? Is the right to a normal life enjoyed and, indeed taken for granted by so many millions, finally mine? Or am I to be saddened by the contents of this official envelope and have to conclude that whilst over the years I have won a few battles, I have indeed finally lost the war? If it is the worst news that I could expect, I dread to imagine what dimension my life will take now. Will my few remaining friends desert me? Will I become an outcast to be shunned or mocked for daring to ask who I am? This document has been in my possession for several days now and even though I am tempted to tear open the envelope, I am still resisting for fear of the discovery that the Passport Office have reneged yet again on their promise that Jane Doe has established her entitlement to a British passport and therefore British citizenship.

We were notified on the 26th May 2006 by telephone from the UK Passport Office in Durham, that the passport for Jane Doe would be issued within ten days and that this was now possible, as they had obtained their own copy of a birth certificate for Barbara Shaw. When they were advised that this could be considered an illegal act (Barbara Shaw has never existed, remember), they replied that they were only establishing that a birth had taken place on the 20th May 1923 in order to enable the issue of the passport!

If I could have one question answered truthfully for me by any person, it would have to be this – how does one become a Jane Doe? In my case it was pure bad luck. Being born in the wrong place, at the wrong time and certainly, the creation of a wrong birth certificate. There is no doubt in my mind whatsoever about that. My whole life has been filled with uncertainty and many, many dreadful memories that will never ever go away. This situation may well have occurred in the lives of others; in differing circumstances maybe, but it will certainly not have been recorded in English legal history. No legal precedent or landmark legislation has ever been recorded, thus the door still remains closed to others in similar situations; those whose births were not properly recorded and their identities tampered with for whatever reason, as mine was.

No other person should have to endure the anguish and torment that I have suffered for too many years but, as I know only too well, the fight has to continue until I and others are granted officially sanctioned and recognised status from the courts, allowing access to our own birth records. In my case these records are closed to public scrutiny until the year 2026. Yes, I was born in 1923, so if I reach the age of 103, I may be lucky yet. What treachery!

The first I knew of the possibility that I might be issued with a British passport was when a week previously to the 26th

May, there had been a telephone conversation with the self-same Passport Office. The content of that discussion was about presenting the birth certificate for Barbara Shaw. Clem notified the official that it had been described as a falsified document, and also the fact that I knew nothing of its existence until I had reached the age of forty-two and had by then six children in a marriage of nineteen years' duration. Still she insisted that I must present it to them. Clem advised me not to and stated to her that we would be aiding and abetting her and ourselves in a crime, as it had been well documented as being a falsified certificate by the Home Office. They previously had traced their records from 1914 through to 1923 and could find no such person as Robert Mark Shaw and no evidence of a marriage either. In the same correspondence we were informed that they had located a marriage between Sydney Shaw and Violet Shaw, formerly Goss, which took place on the 18th July 1919. Clem had actually discovered this information some two years earlier, with the help of the legendary Mormon's Family History Centre at Bulwell, Nottingham. But investigations have failed to confirm the existence of Sydney Shaw, so what does that tell us?

Now, with the support of two Welsh Assembly members and a Welsh MP, and after forty-two years of battling against bureaucracy, can I begin to write the last chapter to my life? Is the document I have longed for all these years, here at last in my hands? I grasp it to my bosom, hoping that my tears this time will be tears of joy; that I can wipe them away in the knowledge that I am at last a real person and say to the world, 'Look... this is who I am!'

Even before I have opened the envelope, I am starting to plan my holiday of a lifetime abroad with Clem. This is something we have only dreamed about so far, but it is what we both deserve after such a long, hard struggle. I do know in my heart of hearts that the contents of this envelope may prove to be yet another disappointment. Things are not always what they seem, and I have been let down like this before. But whatever I find inside, it will be another starting point from which to travel forward to my ultimate goal, or to back-pedal and tackle the hurdles yet again.

I will not reveal the contents, even to myself, until I am ready for that moment. It has been half a lifetime coming and there is no haste; I will savour the sweetness of anticipation for a while longer. I know I have won a battle, but will it be the end of the war? I am indebted and truly grateful to all those who have fought alongside me and spurred me on when I felt like surrendering. To those so-called friends and family members who hoped I would never see this day, I have nothing to say.

Their comments and suggestions have ranged from the merely unhelpful to the damnably obstructive. They have treated me with animosity and contempt for forty years and, I have had to swallow my pride and deal with the indignity of their constant innuendo. The shame of walking out on my family and the reasons behind it are hard enough to bear without being made to suffer that kind of humiliation. But none of us is perfect, and it does take all sorts to make a world; I cannot take responsibility for the actions of others; they must live with their own consciences, as I have had to live with mine. Will I look back on this day and ask myself if it was all worthwhile? I am sure I will, but I cannot yet tell you what my answer will be.

Anticipation and anxious curiosity have kept me in suspense for long enough and the moment of truth has finally arrived. I take the envelope in my hand. The paper knife is nearby. I insert the blade carefully, sliding it along the upper edge.

I can see the contents, and draw them out, trembling slightly as I do so. To me, it is a wondrous sight; a maroon coloured European Union, United Kingdom of Great Britain and

Northern Ireland Passport with the lion and the unicorn in gold lettering.

So at last I have a passport!

I pause for a moment or two; mentally I am telling my friends, foes and family that the Home Office have capitulated and permitted Public Enemy Number One a passport, verifying that I am a British Citizen at the ripe old age of eighty-three. There is jubilation, the cheers are ear-splitting, the phone never stops ringing and we cannot get out through the door for congratulatory messages. What a sight to behold!

In, my dreams.

The reality is very different. My situation has enabled me to know who my friends are and my advice is don't have any 'friends', but get a companion you can trust. As for family, they must now accept the truth about something they have steadfastly refused to acknowledge or deal with. They have offered me no help or support, just belittlement and scorn and this has been a bitter pill for me to swallow. But here at my side, where he has been from day one, is the man I love. I hope they can live with that and find it in their hearts to forgive, for their own sakes.

Now I have to know what name is on that document. I can guarantee there will be tears. But of disappointment, or elation, who knows?

Chapter 24 Settling Down With Clem (1967/68)

Clem had not been living at his flat in Stratford Road all that long when I moved in with him. There were just two rooms at the top of the house and we had the use of very basic facilities. These consisted of an ancient gas cooker, two-bar electric fire, a sink and running water. Bathroom and toilet were shared with the landlord, down one flight of stairs on the middle floor. The bedroom was decorated with washable wallpaper and the condensation was appalling – the walls were simply streaming with vapour droplets and the bedroom felt and smelt damp and musty. A hard winter followed the glorious warmth of the late summer and we actually had icicles forming inside the window frames. The two of us were just content to be together and I daresay we would have been happy in a cave as long as we had each other, but when the cold, damp atmosphere of winter set in, it became intolerable.

Shortly after moving in with Clem, I was lucky enough to find work at the Canadian-owned Gem supermarket, as a shelf-stacker. Clem at that time was working full-time as a window cleaner and we were hoping to be able to save enough money so that we could afford somewhere better to live. I got on well with my co-workers and enjoyed the work, and all was going well until I was sighted by one of George's mates, Harry. They had joined the Navy together and had remained friends ever since. I'm sure that Harry would have been one of the first to be told that I'd forsaken George and the kids. He certainly wasted no time in letting George know that he'd seen me, and one evening as I left work, husband George and son George were waiting for me, and there was no other way they could have known my whereabouts other than through Harry.

They wanted to talk things over and we went into a nearby pub but, as far as I was concerned, there was nothing to discuss. I felt sorry in many ways for walking out on them as I did, but they were not aware of the real reasons behind my decision. Yes, it was true that I had fallen in love with Clem and wanted to be with him, but it was not for purely selfish reasons that I suddenly decided to leave the marital home. There was this other, more perplexing matter that had been on my mind for some time and which still troubled me deeply; something which I had not yet even been able to mention to Clem.

We did have a bit of a discussion over a few drinks, but the conversation was going nowhere. Both men were interested only in getting me to return home and I could see that I was going to find it difficult to get away from them. In the end, so that I could escape, I said that I would think about giving it another try and arranged to see them again a few days later. They accepted this and we left the pub to go our separate ways. To this day I do not know whether they followed me back to Stratford Road, but sometimes I think it is quite probable that they doubled back, discovered where I was living, and then kept a watch on my movements.

When I went into work the following day, I told them I had to leave because of unforeseen circumstances. It was very upsetting. I had become fond of my work mates and they were surprised and saddened, and tried to persuade me to stay, but it was no use. I didn't want to give up my job but I knew that it was necessary for my own peace of mind.

Then one day whilst Clem was working in Loughborough, a visitor came to the flat. The landlord had answered the door and, the caller said he wanted to see Mr. Clements. Knowing I was in, the landlord sent him upstairs, and as I opened the living room door to him, he walked in uninvited, sat down and proceeded to take some documents from his briefcase. These turned out to be divorce papers, which in his capacity as bailiff; he had come to serve on Clem.

As soon as this man entered the room, his whole demeanour changed. I became nervous about his presence, but by this time he had sat down and said he was prepared to wait, even though I had told him that Clem would not be home for some time. He must have stayed more than two hours; I just could not persuade him to go. I was really anxious and, then I mentioned that Clem would be angry if he found another man in the flat and, he would be quite likely to flip and most probably forcibly remove him, (which Clem was more than capable of doing). Anyway, it had the desired effect and, he got up and left, promising to call back the following afternoon.

I was very relieved to see the back of him, I hadn't liked his conversation at all from the moment he barged in. I certainly didn't want to know about his wife and their marital problems; most of all I was offended by his suggestion that I should leave Clem and go and live with him and, I emphatically did not encourage him to discuss his 'undercarriage', which he also referred to as his 'king size three piece suite'!

When Clem came home and I told him we had better leave because his wife was issuing divorce proceedings against him, he was livid. He listened intently to every detail of the disturbing episode and behaviour of this person. His reaction was short and to the point.

"I'll sort it," was all he said, and there was no further discussion on the matter for the rest of the evening. He went off to work early the following morning, having a heavy work schedule to complete within a specified time. He promised to be home before the bailiff returned and, also that he would not allow him to enter our home without a warrant. I knew that Clem meant it; his attitude to this violation of our personal privacy was one of zero tolerance. He just would not put up with it.

However, the bailiff arrived early and Clem was again not at home. I was literally shaking with fright because I knew that in his present mood, Clem would throw him out on his ear, and was more than capable of doing so. This early visit had unsettled and unnerved me, I didn't know what to do, or what was going to happen next. Then, after about thirty minutes, I heard Clem coming up the stairs. I had left the door ajar as I was not at all happy about being alone with this man. When Clem reached the top flight of stairs I spoke to the bailiff so that he would answer and, Clem would be forewarned of his presence. It worked. He came into the room like a bulldozer.

"You are in my home uninvited! I don't know what your game is, but you can just sling your hook right now!"

The bailiff stated that he was going nowhere until he had Clem's signature to the divorce papers being served on behalf of his wife. As I had feared, Clem's anger then boiled over and he physically lifted the man off his feet and ejected him from the room.

"Don't touch me," the man warned. "I'm an ex-policeman!" Clem could not care less if he was King Kong and got hold of him again, this time forcibly propelled him to the top of the stairs, an angrily pointing finger indicating the way down to the street. I think the man was afraid he might be thrown down the stairs; he actually stumbled down them in his haste to get away from Clem. From the window, we watched him run down the street as fast as his legs would carry him, and thankfully never saw him again.

Much later, we learned that he had been sent by Berryman Walker & Slater, solicitors of Friar Lane, Nottingham. They are now Berryman Shacklock and have represented Clem and me many times during our difficulties and are prepared to do so again if we provide them with a five hundred pound retainer to fight for my pension rights. But this is on hold at present; we have paid out too much money already to various well intentioned professional bodies – and still we have nothing to show for it.

The unfavourable conditions at Stratford Road began to play havoc with our health and in January the following year we moved into 2 Chard Street, Old Basford, Nottingham. This property was in an appalling state of disrepair, internally as well as externally, but after a lengthy discussion we decided to move in. Clem promised he would make it into a little palace; we would at least have a place of our own and some privacy, and the rent of one pound fifteen shillings was not going to break the bank. Some dramatic incidents were to take place during our time together there and things happened to us, which I can only describe as being both bizarre and, at times, frightening for both Clem and myself. Events also took place there that completely changed our lives.

Almost two years to the day after accepting that tenancy, we were moving out in favour of another property at 345 Radford Road, Hyson Green, Nottingham. This area, in its hey day, was something of a landmark and rated to be one of the best shopping areas for miles around. The streets were lined with trees and there was an abundance of fine Edwardian houses, some sadly run down, and sought after bedsits of which Clem's brother in law, Arthur, owned several. These were in Noel Street, adjacent to the Nottingham Forest Recreation ground which, once a year, in the first week of October, is given over to the famous Goose Fair event.

However, 345 Radford Road was to be a very short tenancy. Within only a matter of hours of moving in, we had a visit from Social Security in the form of Sgt. Major Etches. A very tall man, sporting a moustache, he was the sternest of his type you could wish to meet. We were surprised by the intrusion and he found us still in our night attire when he came knocking on the door at 8.15 am on the Monday morning, and we were certainly bewildered as to how he found us, but when he stated that he had been to 2 Chard Street we guessed that Celia and Dennis our neighbours had informed him. When Clem opened the door to him, the first words he spoke were, "You've moved then?"

"Yes." Clem's reply was equally terse. "Now get us out if you can."

But before he left, he notified Clem that his benefit was to be cut. Instead of fourteen pounds odd per week, it was now to be ten pounds eighty. This, then, was a taste of the treatment that Clem and I were to expect as we tried to find a home and build a life together. We have managed to do that against all the odds, but it has been an ongoing struggle and, of course, it is by no means over yet.

Chapter 25   Expecting The Unexpected

(My 7th Child At Age 47)

After giving birth to my daughter, Mandy, at thirty nine years of age, I felt that I had played my part in perpetuating the human race and believed my child-bearing days were over. I was therefore somewhat surprised when, at the ripe old age of forty-six, I found myself pregnant for the seventh time. In fact, to say that I was surprised is an understatement – my initial reaction was disbelief, particularly in view of the fact that I had been sterilized in 1964. For this reason, it was some considerable time before it was known what was causing my condition, and I had been diagnosed as suffering from various ailments before a pregnancy test proved positive.

Confirmation of the pregnancy caused Clem and me a lot of heart searching. My health was not that good, and I was warned by the gynaecologist that giving birth could be dangerous for me and I stood a sixty percent chance of losing my life (these were the reasons for being sterilized in the first place!) There was also the very real possibility that I would miscarry. I was offered a termination but that in itself was not without risk. I wanted the baby, so I made up my mind to go ahead with the pregnancy. I thought it would make our union complete – set the seal on it, so to speak. Clem was worried that he might lose me, and although he also liked the idea of our being a proper family, he was less keen than I was. In the end he said that I must make the final choice, that if it were my wish to go ahead with the pregnancy, knowing the possible consequences, he would respect my decision.

Against all the odds, Darran James came safely into the world after a rather topsy turvy pregnancy, the last few weeks of which had been rather traumatic and at times, fear-filled. I already knew that I would produce a boy, from the way that I was carrying. Having reared five daughters and a son, I knew I could not be mistaken. We waited patiently as the time ticked slowly by; everything seemed to be in order. Then one night when Clem was at work driving buses for Nottingham City Transport as a PSV driver, a strange thing happened as I lay in bed in my nightie, reading a book.

I loved to read, especially before bedtime, and I knew that I wouldn't go off to sleep until Clem was safely home. At this time we had still not prepared our bedrooms, so we were using the front room as a bed-sit. I suddenly heard a strange noise coming from the direction of the window. As I looked across, I sat bolt upright with fright. I had seen two hands on top of the casement, slowly sliding the window down. A chill of fear ran down my spine, I felt so sick. I had no idea what the intruder's intentions were; it was passed off at the time by the police as being a Peeping Tom. We learned later that there had been a spate of such incidents in the vicinity. The episode was most upsetting for me, especially as I was nearly six months pregnant at the time.

I screamed as I leapt from the bed and ran next door to my neighbour Dennis and his wife Celia, who called a doctor because of the state I was in. When Clem arrived home a little later to find the house empty, he was naturally alarmed at my absence and, wondering if it was to do with the baby, also went next door to see if Dennis knew anything. He was surprised, but very relieved to find me in there. The doctor had a private word with Clem, advising that he should give up work for a month or so to care for me, because of the risk of miscarriage. This was another blow, as we could not manage without Clem's wages.

As a result, Clem had no choice but to reapply for financial assistance. He was not looking forward to that ordeal at all; the office would be the notorious Hamilton Road Assistance Board, frequently mentioned in newspaper items, once even making the News of the World. It was a frightening, daunting task, one that resulted in a home visit from the department. The officer visited us the following Friday, and naturally we explained exactly what had happened. He seemed sympathetic to our needs and, agreed that we were entitled to two payments, which were to be cashed on the Saturday at the North Street Post Office. He told us that as soon as he returned to the office, the book would be issued and sent out to us that very day. Clem and I felt hugely relieved by this.

Well, Saturday came and went, as did Monday, Tuesday, Wednesday and Thursday. The book finally arrived on the Friday, by this time we were really desperate. We'd had no food for several days and were by now in a dire situation. Phone calls brought no results, apart from the stock reply, 'It's been sent. Report it missing.' On the Thursday, in desperation, Clem borrowed money from the electricity meter, which meant that we all three just about survived; after all, I was supposed to be eating for two.

When the allowance book arrived on the Friday, the envelope was emblazoned with the previous day's postmark, the collection time of 7.30 p.m. They had lied throughout. Clem wouldn't cash it, and took it to Jack Dunnett, our MP, who held a Friday evening surgery on Derby Road, near the Hand & Heart pub. He was very sympathetic and agreed that it was completely out of order. He kept the envelope as proof against the department, and then told Clem to cash the allowance as soon as the Post Office opened on Saturday morning. He stated he would take it up with the office involved. He must have done this almost immediately, because we had a visit from Social Security on the following Monday morning.

The visitor identified himself as the Assistant Manager. I remember he had a greying, full-face beard. Clem was reluctant to let him in to our home but, after much pleading, he did so.

144

The man apologized profusely and gave the excuse that he had fifty staff under his control at the department and it was difficult to know what everyone was doing. Clem advised him to resign. He also told him that the incident had probably caused untold damage to my health and said someone should pay with the loss of their job.

Undeterred, the man then had the audacity to tell Clem that if he took no further action, there would be a grant available to us, as he could see that we were in need of new oil cloth (linoleum) for all the floors, as well as curtains, bedding, utensils, furniture etc., and then there were the requirements of the expected infant... the grant would total two hundred and ninety five pounds (a tidy sum then), but only if we agreed to drop the matter of the allowance book. Clem said no; he considered it a bribe. He said we would then be in their pockets and it would undoubtedly lead to further difficulties, but thinking of all the things we needed just at that time, I was eager to get my hands on the money, and accepted it gladly. With hindsight, of course, Clem was right. He knew that these persons were in local government purely for their own rewards and didn't give a toss about the people they were paid to serve.

Shortly afterwards, when Darran our son was six-months old, we left this property, much to the disapproval of another bullying, self-serving local government officer, whom I shall call Mrs. 'B'. Clem had the misfortune to be interviewed by her at Hamilton Road whilst applying for a grant to enable us to move into 345 Radford Road, Basford, Hyson Green, Nottingham. She forbade the move, arguing that the difference in rent could not be met by Social Security. Clem insisted that the move had been recommended by my doctor on medical grounds, but the woman would not budge even a fraction of an inch. She tried to snatch the rent book from Clem, which he had taken with him as proof of tenancy, and said she was going to instruct the agents to withdraw the tenancy agreement. However, Clem wrestled the rent book from her, so she didn't get the chance to see who the agents were. By then our child, Darran James Clements, was six-months old and it was all haste to move in before the tenancy could be blocked; that was tenancy number two out of what would amount to more than two hundred during our forty year relationship.

Nothing ever seemed to go right for us for long; we were constantly dogged by bad luck one way or another. But it was not too long to wait now before the birth of our child, and that's what helped to keep us going and looking on the brighter side of things. We did manage to obtain some baby clothes – mostly blue, because I was confident that the baby would be a boy. I told Clem, and everyone else, that I was certain of this, our bundle of joy, a healthy boy, arrived on 9th October, 1969, proving me right.

We discovered that legislation had been passed which now permitted an unmarried couple's details to appear on the birth certificate, but after a great deal of argument from the registrar, we eventually signed our names as Mrs. B. Clements and Mr. C. Clements. We were then only allowed to purchase the short version of the birth certificate.

So I had survived a difficult pregnancy in spite of the constant worry and trauma, all of which was absolutely unnecessary. We had a healthy son and we were now a family. We had a home and money to live on. Who knew what the future held for the three of us now? But one thing was for sure; our son would grow up with certain knowledge of his parentage. Unlike his mother.

Chapter 26   Tug Of War Love Child

I have often pondered over that traumatic incident in my early childhood when I was taken from the people and place that I loved. No force was used, but I do believe that it may have been, had there been any resistance to the Halls' demands. Neither my foster mother nor I were able to put up any sort of fight, even though we were both extremely upset. I did feel very let down by this apparent acceptance of the Halls' explanation for taking me, but of course I later came to realize that there was little action that we could have taken against these rough and bullying people.

My life, from the moment I was taken, was never ever the same. There were constant arguments in the family concerning me; accusations levelled at Robert. "Get out!" Violet would scream. "And take that bastard with you." My so called father never did do as she commanded, and I know he had just as difficult a time with her as we did. Yet not once did I see him in an argument with her; I don't know whether this was because he was afraid of her – after all, she was a violent woman, or maybe she had some hold over him... or was it tactical – to run away and live to fight another day? Other men in their right minds, I am sure, would have left her to her own devices and she would certainly have deserved it.

Then I remember something she said to me when she was in one of her rare talkative moods: "You know your dad left me for two years, and one afternoon I had gone to the pictures and when the lights came up he was sat beside me, and I never knew until that moment and that's how we got back together." She never said if this was before I was taken from the cottage at Hitchin, or even if he might have been in prison for some unknown reason; I know he was up to the odd felony now and again – he certainly knew how to break into properties during the times we had to squat. The experiences from those days on the road were to mould me into the kind of person I am today. Too willing by far to please, I was always there with a kind word for anyone in trouble, so that I seemed to attract them to my door. One thing I can say is that they could talk to me knowing I would not betray them; they respected me always. I don't say this out of any feeling of self importance, but I suppose it came from my endless days on the road, and the begging I was forced to do.

I have been told that Henry Hall, the Band Leader, had showmen on his side of the family. One related family is said to live in Mansfield, Nottinghamshire; one day soon we may discover if this is true. I have established that I was a tug-of-war love child. The battle was between a wealthy woman, who wanted to adopt me on the one hand, and Violet and her sister, my aunt Lily, on the other. If this was so, could it have been the couple at the cottage who adopted me through the Ward of Court Order I had been placed under? Anyone interfering with this order would face dire consequences and suffer the might of the court for disobeying that order. Wards of Court are interesting individuals, especially those of the weaker sex, and will often form a favourite character for novelist and playwright alike.

If I had been abandoned at some early point of my life, I would have become a Ward of Court. Other reasons could have been a refusal to register my birth, when the court would take the responsibility upon themselves to name me, so it could be that neither Violet, nor Lily or even Robert himself were to blame, but the court, acting in my best interests in the belief that it would sort itself out. Another ecclesiastical word springs to mind and that is postulation; those who hid my identity were biding their time with the premise that an explanation could be found to save them embarrassing questions in relation to why a person would be issued with false credentials. Surely they must have been awake to the probability that at some stage of my life I was bound to discover this enigma which existed concerning my birth and would want to know more of who had the power to alter my birth record to suit their own ends, and the reasons why?

Since I learned that I was not Barbara Hall but had suddenly become Barbara Shaw, I have pursued this discrepancy relentlessly and vigorously. For four decades it has been to no avail but at last I am gaining ground in that I have just received from HMRC National Insurance Contributions Office, Newcastle upon Tyne, a request as to whether I have any idea when I was born; also... have I been given any NI numbers that don't belong to me and do I have any record of any of the NI numbers? Possibly a breakthrough, but first things first; after all, fourteen years of pension rights are at stake. There will be no response from either myself or my solicitor on this issue; an affidavit will be sworn that I do not know how I came to have nine NI numbers. I did not request any of them and had no part in their issue, so it is not my problem. I am fighting for the pension rights that I am entitled to and to learn of the one NI number that would have secured my entitlement. I believe as a married woman my entitlement should have been based on my husband's contributions – after all I could not work as I was a housewife and mother of six, and accordingly my pension would have been taken care of under the 1953 National Insurance Act. Whether I was a kidnap victim doesn't come into the equation; when I married on 5th May 1945 in good faith, I had absolutely no idea that the name of Hall had been procured upon me by deception. That name had been prevalent with me for seventeen years.

I had not been allowed to take any part in the conversation between Robert Mark Hall and the registrar in

Nottingham prior to my marriage at the Bristol registry office. Am I now to believe that my circumstances were contrived... that I am such an enigma that no one will ever be permitted to know whatever it is that is being suppressed under ecclesiastical law? My life is and has always been steeped in turmoil and secrecy; the question is, do I have the means to put an end to the mystery that I am enshrined in? My answer is maybe not, but that is not for the want of trying. If I were a batsman I would be on course for a marathon innings... how else can I explain my dilemma; will I be run out at the end? I have not been caught or bowled out yet.

To all intents and purposes my real life has been permitted to pass me by under the name of secrecy and conspiracy, I have achieved some success, so my efforts have not all been in vain, I have a wonderful person for a husband and I truly couldn't wish for more, but I know there is more to my life than just a story, there is the compulsion that drives me on, either to the bitter... or, I hardly dare hope for... the happier conclusion. The moment the truth was upon me, I had to do some serious thinking. My life was never going to be the same; it would be a life that I was not prepared to continue with. I knew I would be commanded to forget about it all, and yet, from that moment on, I knew I could not spend all my life in obscurity... being a nobody, a non-person. For three years I nursed this hurt, trying to bring some normality into my life, but it didn't happen, and I was in a state of suspension. Everything was in slow motion; my days were endless, I was not sleeping, it was all telling on my health. But at that time I had no one I could turn to or confide in.

I don't blame my husband for his complacency. I was not fully aware of what had transpired, the whole matter was extremely complex. I knew that he was never a man of many words; I was terribly starved of conversation. My marriage had been a whirlwind relationship – that is a fact which I fully and unequivocally accept. I had given no serious thought to what I was doing and gladly gave my hand in marriage for better or worse. Anything was better than the hell-hole I was suffering with the Halls at that time and marriage was, I suppose, an escape.

There is no mistaking the likeness between Violet, my so called mother and me, but there is also no mistaking my likeness with my Aunt Lily, so, in concluding that they are both kin I am halfway to solving this conundrum. One or the other was my biological mother, but how to prove which one? So I now know I have a mother, whichever of the two, but until I have the certainty of knowing which one, a big chunk of my life is missing. Will it be forever? Please, no. But now I have to give it my best shot and undivided attention to try to trace my biological father; no stone (nor headstone) will be left unturned, unexamined, until I have his name and I can expose him for the hurt he has caused me.

It was once told to me in the utmost secrecy – and I had to be sworn to secrecy, that my biological father died in 1972 but not in this country. I would not have revealed this trust, but I cannot for the life of me recollect who it was that entrusted me with this information. However, I don't think I shall be looking for someone who died in that year in another country; there are too many death registers to open. That will remain a closed chapter.   My attention will not be diverted away from the genealogical line of descendancy of Sydney Shaw, William Goss, Henry Robert Hall (BBC bandleader) and Robert Mark Hall, all key players in the drama that is my identity crisis. My story is a shameful tale; certainly unusual – bizarre even, and astonishingly incredible… but true. I have been the victim of an elaborate confidence trick, spanning eight decades, and I think that takes some beating.

Chapter 27   Haunted By My Past

The worst part about my situation is that I have had to live with it constantly. Some of the more traumatic episodes of my life are best forgotten about, but being able to bury these bad memories is not easy. In fact, for me, it is impossible and I feel as though I am living in a shadow of the past, wanting to break out into the sunlight to live a normal life and leave the horrors of the past behind me forever.

Until I can explain my life entirely, I can never expect to live as a normal person can. What happened to me happened; there is no denying it. It is just a shame that I had no knowledge of it until it was far too late. None of my doing, and yet the pressure has been upon me to explain matters that I know nothing about – when they took place, or who was responsible. The onus rests on me, ultimately; being considered as a responsible adult, the burden of proof obviously comes home to roost on my doorstep and I cannot escape that fact.

I could have challenged my so-called parents when I reached the age of consent… in my case this would have been when I reached the age of twenty-one. But I was naïve and ignorant of such matters then, besides which, it would have been most unwise of me to show such audacity. Consider, for a moment, my upbringing… I would have faced the jaws of a lion rather than incur the wrath of my so-called mother. She was a daunting prospect to anyone who dared to challenge her; there were few who would not cringe at her vicious outbursts, so what could I, the meek and mild child who dare not say boo to a goose, do about it?

Then I tell myself to reflect on what I know so far and no matter how much Clem is helping me to uncover my past, I am so impatient with myself. I know that I have been stupidly naïve throughout my life, to have not discovered until it was far too late, the aspects that are of vital importance to everyone... their parental background. And then to discover that a dark family secret has been hidden and buried in order to prevent any vestige of truth from ever emerging lest dire consequences result – well, who would not feel timid against the might of those responsible for keeping the past hidden?

Then, at other times, I will change course and ask myself whether I am reading this all wrong. What if, perchance, I was placed in a foster home with people who were akin to the church, for my own good and to protect me from whatever dark deeds were to blame? This would surely be reasonable... the right and proper action to take by those having responsibility for me. Then yet another question poses itself: what if my problem stems from a similar difficulty concerning Violet, my so called mother? Could it be that all that has happened to me is a throw back from her background – was she who she thought she was, or was she told to be who she was – just a passing fancy plucked from the air, as I was? Violet lies at rest in her grave now, but still I would like to be able to say I loved her in spite of the way I was treated, and considered her to be the only mother I ever really knew.

I now know how important it is to me to know the origins of my birth... to have a birth certificate and marriage certificate that would hold up in a court of law as being the official recognition of who I am. Sadly, in my case, although I have the respective documents, neither of them relate to me, and so it's down to me, with Clem's help, to endeavour to find out why. I suppose, but can have no way of knowing, that if the circumstances of my birth were in some way similar to my mother's birth, then the knock-on effects have clearly misaligned my whole family as well as Clem and our son. After all, I know nothing of my mother's background other than what she has herself told me. Throughout my days of travelling with them, I met very few relatives that I can identify by name. Any questions I did pluck up courage to ask were always met with disdain, or, put another way, they were not to be answered for specific reasons, so it was intimated that I was too young to understand, and felt a swipe round the ears for daring to ask.

Growing up into normal society was hard; very hard, I would not wish it on my worst enemy, and where I found the strength that got me through it all, I will never know. Living and fending for myself helped but no person's life should be riddled with doubt and uncertainty and I sympathize with anyone who has had to endure a likewise situation. However, some facts are slowly emerging and we are able, at last, to ask certain questions that cannot be ignored.

The one very important question is: how did I manage to attain nine National Insurance numbers? We know for certain that a person holds one for life. Clem and I have challenged these numbers over many years and it has been suggested on occasions that we were partners in crime! Surely our ruse would have been detected and we would have met with the might of the courts and sentenced forthwith to deter anyone else from attempting to defraud our benefit State (a sad sign of the times is that it has become commonplace now... falsified NI numbers are worth a mint). We never did and never would – it never occurred to us to do such a thing.

So how did I manage to cheat the system by acquiring so many numbers? One thought crossed my mind; it could well have been that I was never in the system to begin with. This 'omission' could have occurred to rectify my problem of being born into the world without an identity in the first instance. My first reaction was that I was the subject of an intended cover-up, which has been hinted at frequently. Again this is all supposition – guessing is okay for some, but not for me. In 1956, shortly after the birth of my fifth child, Carol, I stood formally accused that I did on the 24th day of September of that year, almost certainly suffering from post-natal depression, abandon my family. I subsequently turned up on the Isle of Wight and then proceeded to find employment and obtain a National Insurance number in the name of Barbara Goss. This is stated in writing to me from the Pension Service through the offices of a high-ranking official. This written confirmation was sent to that official's office claiming that I, Barbara Hall, had no maiden name and no verified date of birth and also that he was concerned about Jane Doe's missing identity. How it was possible for all this to take place without my knowledge, and then to stand accused some twenty years later is beyond me; why would I, a married woman of eleven years with five young children to look after dare to attempt such a thing?

Governments move in mysterious ways; they never let their left hand know what the right hand is doing. Moving the goal posts is another way that I would describe my situation and the secrecy surrounding it. Will I ever score anything in my life while I still have a chance to put it in order? Not in my lifetime, I fear. It is impossible to calculate how many times the real issue has been evaded. Why am I such a secret? Why is no one permitted to know? All these questions and more are ever present and always will be. They do have answers; we know that other people out there are still enduring endless battles to secure their futures; well, start with theirs if mine is too unhealthy to tackle, but put our lives in order by granting us our inherent right to the truth and nothing but the truth.

I could come to terms with my outrageous predicament if I could ascertain whether I was an adopted child, or even better still if I had been made a Ward in Chancery. This would throw some light onto why I have been kept so much in the dark about the early years of my life. It has been stated that there are only five others besides myself in this situation. In a way it is comforting to me – or would that be too much to hope for? It would give me a nice sense of not feeling so alone if I knew others were also doing battle over their identities. I am still waiting for clarification of whether my marriage at the Bristol Registry Office on 5th May 1945 is legal. My! Is someone deciding to put the records straight after so many years of ignoring my plight? I hope it is that marriage they are referring to and not my two bigamous marriages to Clem. These two marriages were brought about by a sense of desperation and confrontation. This is why we took on so many solicitors; after all, if anyone can do it, they can… or so we are led to believe. In our own circumstances we discovered they didn't have a clue; either that or someone else was pulling their strings. We have the dossier that is a damning indictment against them. Some were more helpful, up to a point – until they knew what they were letting themselves in for.

It was at this time that Clem became ruthless, almost cruel in his approach to solve this mystery of my being. He refused to be fobbed off with silly explanations from solicitors who should have known better than to try to hoodwink him into believing there was no resolve to my having been provided with a fabricated birth certificate. He believed it was a crime at its inception and so did others in the legal profession; after all, a crime is a crime, no matter the passing of time. He soldiered on regardless of whose cages he rattled, which brought results to a degree that he was being listened to for a change. Hence the latest correspondence from the General Registry Office, Southport dated 2nd November 2007 and addressed to Ieuan Wyn Jones, Assembly Member for Ynys Mon, which thanks him for his letter dated 23rd October 2007 regarding his constituent, Barbara Hall. (Barbara Hall has never been his constituent; Ms Jane Doe has.) Ms Hall is concerned that her marriage may not be legal owing to complications with her birth certificate. In our research, we have not been able to trace a single piece of proof that this is my birth certificate and until we do, I will never accept that it is mine or has any bearing on my identity.

Chapter 28 My Life Is A Conspiracy

My supposed mother claimed me, stating that I was her child, when I was nearly five years old. I have come to realise many things about this event, and as I now approach my eighty-fourth birthday, I have more sympathy towards her since she passed away, taking to the grave the secret of my birth and the mysterious registration details. There is much that I still need to find out; more about Violet and her early life and circumstances, which I feel would provide vital clues.

There have been many crises in my life, from my earliest memories to the present time, and most of these disturbing incidents can be traced back to my flawed birth certificate, and the fact that I do not know who I really am, legally or ancestrally. I have always felt that there was a conspiracy of silence in my family, and I was the sole subject of it. Its purpose was to deprive me of ascertaining any knowledge concerning certain aspects of my identity.

It was also a conspiracy of power; those given power are able to hide, distort and manipulate the truth, always to their own advantage. These persons with their tools of control and influence had a vested interest in preventing the secret of my biological parentage emerging. But why? A truthful explanation would have solved many problems for me, and prevented a great deal of misery and heartache over the years.

There are many others out there who have likewise discovered details of their births that just do not add up. What are they doing about it? Absolutely, nothing. For what valid reason would our births be subject to the Official Secrets Act? I have learned that in my case, any interested parties connected with the media have been served with D Notices to prevent the publication of any 'sensitive' details concerning my birth. In recent years these notices have been referred to as Public Interest

Immunity (PII), so you can see that I do live a life which is definitely conspired against. After a while it is possible to shrug off the fear that this causes, even though I live in anticipation of another sinister episode to replace the one before it. However, it means that I can never drop my guard and it just becomes a constant battle; a nightmare that is never going to go away.

I relive my life's events in every detail from the day I was taken, to this present day, and I will never relent. I will never give up my search for more knowledge about my life; knowledge that is kept hidden well away from me and from anyone who dares to ask about my origins, even though we have an inherent right within the shores of this land known to all as the United Kingdom. The custodians of these records have a duty to serve; that is why they are referred to anomalously as public servants. I cannot think of any occasion when I could honestly say that they have served me. In fact they have compounded my situation by evading the truth, always boxing clever to avoid answers from which I might glean some clue about what took place all those years ago.

I worked out that the only plausible answer to my plight was that I must have been a tug of war love-child. I think I suspected from an early age that I was an unwanted or 'born the wrong side of the blankets' child. However, the fact that I was apparently fostered and didn't know these so-called parents until I was nearly five years old, leads me to suspect a quite different explanation.

I now believe that I was made a Ward in Chancery (Ward of Court), the reason for which I may discover when my solicitor makes an application for my birth record. Ordinarily, most people believe that I am referring to the details entered on my birth certificate. That is not so; a birth certificate is the second record of one's birth, the first one being the moment a new-born draws its first breath. The hospital, or midwife's record is the one to which I refer. These are accurate and record the mother's name, the weight of the child and the details of the delivery (in my case, a forceps delivery, according to what Violet once told me when she was in one of her drink-fuelled talkative moods).

The day I was bundled into the 'Varda' wagon all those years ago is etched into my memory so indelibly that it never can be erased, it is almost like my own shadow that follows me everywhere and cannot be got rid of until I can cast a strong enough light to chase it into a corner. This is the shadow of my past which is with me constantly but, one day, I know and am very confident, that I will dispel this shadow when my case is brought before the courts to establish through the midwife's records (Sarah Ellen Wheatley) once and for all, my true origins and identity. We are positive that these records have the information that we seek, which will dispel all the myths and doubts that have built up over the years. There is quite a catalogue of uncertainties which I can no longer live with. I know the truth is out there to provide the answers that will most definitely put my house in order. If it does, it will not of course rectify this great wrong that has been procured upon me, but it will at least stifle and snuff out any further progression of this legacy of lies that I have unwittingly inherited, and prevent its progression to future generations.

The outcome of my official identity as Ms. Jane Doe has to be verified against the name I relinquished before taking on my adopted name, as well as tying in with my National Insurance and NHS numbers. Those presently recorded as my numbers actually belong to others. This should be a simple procedure whereby I produce evidence to substantiate my position so that the matter can be rectified. The process should eliminate eight NI numbers and four NHS numbers; after all who would want to progress through life to the issue of a passport based on seven different surnames, nine NI numbers and five NHS numbers? I ask you… is it likely that I or anyone is ever likely to know who I am.

With this resolve out of the way I could establish that my identity has been tampered with, either deliberately or, more intriguingly, by way of a cover-up. The latter is probably the most probable explanation of this long running saga which appears to have no ending. If capitulation is a way forward, then I will not be the one to give in; those responsible have to be the ones to make the moves to put it right, even at this late stage. My life so far has passed me by; freedom is a word with no meaning. I would like to live a little, most certainly travel a little and… well, just enjoy myself a little. I don't think I am asking too much at eighty-four years of age; the normal pleasures of life that most take for granted have been denied to me because, for all these years, the truth has been hidden away, swept under the carpet with the dust of my life.

My life has been a tragedy from the moment I was born; not a tragedy waiting to happen, but one which was predictable and controlled from the outset. It is curious to say the least. If the midwife's records establish my birth date as Whit Sunday, 20th May 1923 – a historical day in the political calendar when the Prime Minister resigned from office, why was it that my mother never once made me aware that this was my official birth dates? Surely one would want their child to know if they had been born on such an auspicious occasion. Unfortunately, I didn't learn of this fact until after she had sunk into dementia. By that time any amount of questions would be of no purpose, and my relationship with Lita, my sister, had soured to the extent that she yelled down the phone that her mother had suffered enough, and don't ring again, before hanging up.

I now wonder if this is because of a visit from the police after Clem and I had pulled off our second bigamous marriage on Valentine's Day 1992. It was leap year and I had proposed to

Clem; he told me he was unable to turn down such an offer and we tied the knot on 14th, February that year. Five weeks later, we were arrested and then released on bail until 2nd April. The arresting officers informed us that they would be paying Robert and Violet a visit in Nottingham. Could it have been this visit that brought about Robert's demise? I shall never know; Lita refused to tell me, which leads me to think an official visit from the police may have muddied the waters again. I was given the impression she never wanted to speak to me again; I can live with that... we were never close. What I say to her now is that I only hope she can live with herself.

Christine, my niece, notified us of the visit through contact with the West Midlands Police. I still think it uncannily coincidental that the police knew exactly where to find Robert and Violet, let alone Clem and me, considering that we did not use our Birmingham address when we married bigamously for the second time. I am as confident as one could be that Violet was not my biological mother; I know now that she made up stories when I was a young girl. One time, when I was brushing her hair, she told me that Lily her sister was barren. She also told me that when they were in school they had to wear different coloured ribbons in their hair so that the teachers could tell them apart as they were so alike they could have been mistaken for twins. That must have been a lie; Clem's research into family history puts Violet's birth in 1900 and Lily's in 1904. Is it possible, though, that their lives could have been fiddled, as mine has been? And who dare we mention because of their involvement? We will have to wait and see; one day, perhaps, all will be revealed in these chapters.

Chapter 29   Lady Barbara

Right from the start, that is, from the day when I was taken away by Robert and Violet, I was ordered never to call Violet 'Mother'. I don't know that I ever wanted to. She didn't treat me as any normal mother would; there was no love or affection; no caring or cuddling. But Violet was always calling me Lady Barbara. No not in any endearing way, not like Henry Hall did, when he sat me on his knee during his visits. She used the term in a derisory way, usually curling her upper lip as she spoke the words.

Violet's sister Lily also called me Lady Barbara, but she was always very caring and loving towards me. I remember Robert taking me to a huge country house on several occasions. I never knew whose it was, but it has been asked of me whether I knew if Lily also visited there. I do not know. It would help me to remember more if I had been able to locate where it is; it may jog my memory as it did when I found the cottage in Hitchin where I had been taken from. The whereabouts of this fine house would, I am sure, put another piece into the jig-saw that my life has become.

There is no bitterness left in me now, in spite of what has happened to me over the years. There is no longer any time or room in my life for animosity, or revenge. I am not that kind of person, but who could blame me if I were; haven't I just cause to want my own back for the years of torment and turmoil I have suffered because of the mystery surrounding my birth?

There is no denying that my life has been ruined because of a State secret. The evidence lies in the many cover-ups and also in the fact that my actual birth records had been closed to public scrutiny until the year 2038, but that has recently been amended to 2026. (They probably think it a fairly safe bet that if I am still around when I am one hundred and three years old, I will have either given up my quest, or will be incapable of continuing with it!) I am sure that the information held in these midwifery archives would establish categorically who my real parents were, but I am told they are closed to prying eyes and that is final.

It is also the final furlong for me. I am in my twilight years and my life has almost run its course, but I would like the record to be put straight if that is at all possible, for the benefit of future generations. I don't want them to inherit the very same legacy that I did; all the same, I feel sure that it will be many decades after I am gone before this mystery is finally put to rest.

A voyage down memory lane is something we all take from time to time. I have journeyed many times down my memory lane, and the journey always begins on the day I was bundled unceremoniously into the "Varda" wagon on that warm spring day when I was almost five years old. In fact, I was literally snatched away from the couple who had cared for me so lovingly. I would dearly love to know more about the reasons for being placed in their care in the first place.

Sixty-nine years after I was taken from their cottage I retraced my steps and, with a stroke of good fortune, I stepped back into my past and came alive again, living and rejoicing my achievement of what I had thought was an impossible dream. I was certain that no one had ever believed my story of a little girl, dressed for summer, who had been taken from her guardians to begin another life as a gypsy girl; a life so alien it would mock and haunt her to her dying day. No one should be compelled to suffer such an indignity in life.

So I continue to journey down my memory lane. I have such a compelling need to find the truth that it dominates every aspect of my life; every fibre of my body. This compulsion is almost unbearable to live with at times and I know in my heart that I could have endured none of it without the devotion and dedication of Clem, my remarkable husband. He is as possessed with unveiling the truth as I am, and will leave no stone unturned until the mystery of my birth is solved. The incredible indiscretions of my biological father will, one day, be revealed for the entire world to witness.

The last time I saw my Aunt Lily would have been when I was about twelve years of age. She played a big part in my life and I recall something she said to me which has disturbed me most throughout my life. It was unexpected, but had a profound effect on me.

"Barbara," she said, "You will weep many a bitter tear before you get much older, but always remember that you have…"

The words that followed, I dare not reveal here; I have been forced to 'forget them' because of reprisals if I utter them, but one day when I have more evidence, I solemnly promise that I will reveal those words. I will lay them bare and be damned to those who would hold my life to ransom for eight decades to safeguard protocol.

My real life has passed me by. The substitute life that I have chosen for myself is far better than the one foisted upon me, much better than anything that has gone before, but it could have been so much better without the life sentence of uncertainty and deprivation that has been passed on to me for daring to ask, 'Who am I?' One day, I hope that my life will be as normal as one would expect and be entitled to in a modern society and, whilst I have great hopes and expectations for my future, this will give me the strength to continue asking questions and demanding answers until I get the result, the key which will unlock the prison gates and finally set me free from this living hell. I hope, as I continue to trawl the archives – back issues of newspapers, the electoral rolls, and the records of births, marriages and deaths, I will turn up one vital document which will dispel once and for all the mist of uncertainty that has veiled the truth and kept the secrets locked away from me.

There are so many disturbing facts to my life which will not add up and, until they do, I remain an orphan of the storm. So I cannot give up; I have to progress ever onward. Gradually, painfully slowly, I will go on piecing together every piece of information, every detail that I can remember, no matter how trivial it seems, in order to reach a conclusion and finally understand why my life went terribly off course. If my case had found its way into the courts by whatever means, and I had been found guilty, in spite of overwhelming documentation that I knew would establish my innocence, then that would have been described as a miscarriage of justice. But I cannot get into court for love or money, even though technically I continue to break the law on a daily basis.

When I changed my name by Deed Poll, I saw this as my first opportunity to put my life into some semblance of order. It would be required of me to notify family, all departments dealing with pension and benefit claims, as well as the Supreme Court and the London Gazette. I was required by law to do that, which I did, and yet I am still locked in conflict with the officials who made these demands. Apparently it wasn't achieving the result that they desired, so they tried again and again to persuade me to give them more information. But until they give me the answers to my questions, I am still unable to make any further comment for fear of incriminating myself.

Now, all of a sudden, I find that time has rolled on to my eighty-fourth year. How could they put anyone through such a nightmare for daring to ask, 'Who am I?' I should not have to ask this question, and should not have been placed in a situation that seems to imply that I am the guilty one. My circumstances are the result of the actions of my so called parents, whoever they may have been. If it had happened to me as a young child living now in these modern times, there would be protection established in law but unfortunately, that has all come too late to benefit me. The only thing being protected as far as I can see is the big secret surrounding my birth.

I feel that I have reached a milestone, which prompts me to ask myself how much further down the road I want to travel. I must be careful where I permit my road to take me; each journey into my hurtful past takes its toll and I am so tempted to throw in the towel. I know that I would like to put the whole affair behind me for the very last time, no more questions, no more answers, but that would be accepting defeat and admitting failure. I have come this far, and I will stay the course. With the right frame of mind and Clem beside me, I am sure I will cover the distance and who knows; along the way I may find a court willing to help me to prove that I am a person with a human and legal right to an identity.

It will have been a very long walk to freedom, but I think I will have earned it. Everything that has been thrown at me I've thrown back, and guess what? Not so much seems to be coming in my direction now. Either they are running out of ammunition, or I am successfully repelling their missiles. Or both. Dare I hope that a resolve is in sight on both sides of the fence or will it be that the big secret is destined to be buried with me as it was with my so-called parents, whom I knew as my mother and father, even though I have discovered they were not? Irrespective of whom they were and the legacy I inherited from them, I loved them both. That may be difficult to understand, but isn't that what is expected of us? Should we not try to find forgiveness in our hearts, no matter how cruel the circumstances we find ourselves in? I say, very positively, yes! But, please, are we not also entitled to know the truth, to make the burden a little easier to bear?

Chapter 30   Hard Times

Times seemed to be always hard as far as the Hall family was concerned and any money which came into their possession burned holes either in Robert's gambling or Violet's boozing pocket. When the war years took the men folk away to fight and brought rationing, everyone felt the pinch and had to do the best they could for their families. It was a desperately difficult time for some of the larger families who were already struggling to make ends meet.

Robert decided that rather than go and fight for his country or even take up some useful work, he would adhere to the habits of a lifetime and conserve most of his energy by sponging from his fellow men. At this time we were living in Manning terrace in the St, Anne's area of Nottingham. Robert acquired a pair of crutches and would go begging in the streets, often appearing with a placard round his neck, proclaiming to be a veteran of the Great War. I was made to go with him to add pathos to his plight, the pair of us could often be seen around the market place in Matlock, Derbyshire. When I bring these memories to mind, I live again the moments of shame and indignity that I was forced to bear.

There have always been knock-on effects throughout my life, mysteries that I cannot cast from my mind, and I ask myself repeatedly, why did it all happen to me? I never went out of my way to confront anyone concerning my iniquitous situation, and for years I kept it all bottled up inside me, never daring to breathe a word to a living soul. In fact my own soul was in torment, afraid for my very life and those closest to me, my family. I had no friends. This introspectiveness was a by-product of my experiences, which had taught me better than to ask anything of anyone, particularly about my past ? this was meant to be dead and buried forever. But how was that possible, how could I forget such a life? I knew the day would come when I would have to stand up and challenge those who decreed that this vital information be kept from me. One day I would have to find my voice, stand up and say, look this is all about me, it concerns me and I have a right to know the answers to my questions. How otherwise would they go away and leave me to find out for myself?

Why was I the one to inherit a legacy of lies? This deception knows no bounds; with each little nudge, the snowball grows even larger, but when we finally reach the top of the long, steep hill and give it that final push, God help anybody standing in its way as it gathers speed.

Inevitably, this well guarded secret had to be exposed, not only for my sake but those closest to me. Time should have healed the heartache I felt when I walked out nearly forty years ago, but it has only deepened the wound by lengthening the blade of deceit. And the longer it continues, the more it will hurt. Am I to endure this torment until the day I die?

Do I regret walking out? Emphatically no! This is not because I have become hardened over the years and ceased to care, far from it. No, it was because I felt unworthy of my family and I thought that by staying, it would just perpetuate the lie and bring a stain of disgrace upon them all that would spread eventually into deep hatred. The decision was mine, and mine alone, but no one of us is wholly to blame. The responsibility sits squarely on the doorstep of those in authority who have consistently evaded the issue in the hope that it would one day cease to be. Well, the news is that it has not gone away, nor has it diminished; it is still very much in evidence.

When I was handed a birth certificate stating that I was someone other than the person I had always thought I was, and not (indeed never was) Barbara Hall, I had no ideas about how to put my life back on track forty years too late. The shock of it was devastating. How was I to deal with it? How would anyone deal with such a revelation, such a magnificent deception? Who were the perpetrators, and for what reasons? I ask myself time and again, how could I have been so naïve that I never suspected anything all those years whilst bringing up a family in such hard times?

My whole life dramatically changed when I discovered that my name was really Barbara Shaw. The discovery of this birth certificate allegedly relating to me, some forty years after its inception, has not only ruined my own life, but also the lives of those I loved and cherished. To my family I say again, the blame does not lie with me, and if only you had listened to me when I tried, so often, to talk to you about it; if you could have just given me a fair hearing, it might have been possible to salvage something from the wreckage. As it was, none of you wanted to know. Not your problem, why should you have to be bothered with any of it? The millpond was calm enough until I tossed a stone into the middle and caused the ripple that was to become a tidal wave.

Your complacency, at a time when I desperately needed emotional support, led to me taking the action that I did. Did I listen to my heart or my head? As soon as I realised the implications of that birth certificate, my instinct was to shield and protect you from my past; I was as innocent as you all were, but I was the one who would ultimately carry the lifelong stigma created by that one act of treachery by persons as yet still unknown. Rightly or wrongly, I did what I thought was best for all of us at the time, and I do not regret it. But please don't imagine for one moment that it was painless. From my heart I can tell you that I have never felt pain like it.

What is past is done and you must get on with your lives as you see fit. I'll never know whether I did right or wrong; I daresay it might have been handled better. But be certain of this

- one day the truth will out. Someone, somewhere, will want to get to the bottom of this mystery and the conspiracy that has dominated my life for more than forty years. I have had to live with the implications of this mind-bending revelation and sometimes it has been almost unbearable; certainly it is not easy for me to describe in words.

I make no excuses; I have remained silent for far too long, afraid that I would upset someone's life as I pursued my own selfish quest for the truth, and I am adamant in repeating that I am not sorry for leaving as I did. I had warned you all often enough that, one day, you would come home to an empty house, that I would be gone, never to return. You chose to ignore me and the rest is history. It is just possible that I may have returned, but that is pure speculation. After meeting up with Clem that was never going to happen; with him I was sure I could resolve my iniquitous situation. It is no fault of Clem's that I have not yet been successful, I am amazed that he has selflessly battled so hard and so long on my behalf. I am sure no one could have given it more effort.

When I left you all I had no idea what I was letting myself in for, but I have paid the price for what have been called my dastardly actions. Then I ask myself why should I feel so guilty? None of this is of my making. I am innocent of all the charges made; how could I possibly have known that there were those hell-bent on preventing me from ever uncovering any detail concerning my past? There have been many players in this cloak and dagger game, which commenced the moment I walked out. I was not to be allowed any privacy in my new found life, there was to be no respite, as a result, I and my loved ones have suffered unimaginable indignities. How is this possible in these days of political correctness with its rigid anti-discrimination laws? Freedom of Information Act? Excuse me, what freedom has there been in my life? Have I been permitted to go where I liked, to take a holiday in the sun whenever the desire betook me? When have I ever felt free? As I recall, never; the eternal prisoner is how I describe myself. Yes!

We all from time to time endure hard times, they are part of life and we learn to live with them. Some of us are more fortunate than others in this respect, but we all take our places in society and bond in whatever way we feel appropriate. It's about life's struggles and helping each other to deal with them. I hope now with all my heart and soul that with the granting of a passport supporting my entitlement to British citizenship, I can begin to experience some normality in life, to feel as if I belong somewhere at last. Surely that is not too much to expect in my twilight years? And, with all the confidence I can muster, I sincerely hope and pray for a final and legally recognised marriage to the man who has shown exceptional courage, understanding and extreme valour throughout my life-long ordeal. Without Clem, I know I would not have made it this far.

If there is anyone else who can claim to have suffered a similar or even worse fate than I have, then let us stand united and fight this system that has suppressed our rights as well as our freedom. Why should we cower alone, afraid to speak out for fear of upsetting those whose intention is only to silence our cry for freedom? An ocean of water has flowed under the bridge since I was born eighty-three years ago; surely after such a long period of time, does it really matter so much, whom my father was? I certainly don't care and don't really want to know. What good can it do me now? No, all I ask is for someone to admit that mistakes have been made concerning my identity; to acknowledge the emotional cost to me as well as compensating me for the loss of my pension rights so that I can pick up the threads of my life and make the most of what is left of it.

Or, alternatively, shall I have to press on and pursue further investigation into why I have been compelled to accept a falsified birth certificate as well as erroneous (and numerous) National Insurance numbers, none of which can be explained to me by those whose job it is to regulate and control such matters?

Now I am required to give an explanation as to how it all happened. The only reply I am able to give is this: how could I have been so naïve as to let any of it happen? My early life has been wasted, my first marriage was a sham, to all intents not even a marriage at all. I must be the dumbest woman on this planet, needing help so badly.

I am afraid to reveal all my suspicions but, for everything to be understood, I would need to disclose the identity of the man whom I believe was my biological father. Fairly recently I have been informed by a reliable source that I am unique in that I am one of only six in this country with my kind of 'pedigree'. I was also told that my real father died in 1972, but not in this country. I do not know whether there is any truth in any of this, or whether I should pass it off as hearsay and disregard it. Speculation of this kind could run amok and some constraint must be exercised; the matter is highly sensitive and we would be entering unknown territory. Any action taken, therefore, would have to be acceptable to all concerned. At the moment it is academic, as I do not have available resources to investigate the possibility further. But it certainly has me thinking…

Chapter 31   44, Bidford Road

I have to say that out of the countless addresses we have lived at, this was the worst I can ever remember. Disaster seemed to descend upon us the moment the tenancy was signed over. We had been permitted to move into this property on 13th January, 1986 after the council had removed the grilles from the windows and doors and restored the water supply, which had been turned off for winter protection. Prior to moving in we had been homeless for more than a year, which qualified us for immediate re-housing. Another reason we were accelerated to the top of the housing list was that it had been discovered in the previous October that I had lung cancer, when I had undergone a scan for a bone disease. Fortunately for me this was a wrong diagnosis and the scar tissue showing on my lungs was probably due to exposure to dangerous chemicals whilst working at the bomb filling factory during the war years. (Digressing for a moment, it is curious to note that, conveniently, there are no records of me having worked for the war effort. However I do know I worked there, hopefully there are those who can support my claim, one day soon I will turn up crucial evidence to substantiate my claim.)

The day we moved in with our belongings, which at that time was virtually what we stood up in; we had to move straight out again. This was because someone, probably the previous tenants, had removed the plumbed-in washer, complete with its fixings, all unnoticed by the council who had failed to observe the two holes left in the pipe work under the sink. There had also been a burst pipe in the loft during a recent cold spell, so we were moving into a house that was flooded, cold, damp and completely un-inhabitable. Not an auspicious start, after our long spell of homelessness.

1985 was a memorably cold year, and I might easily have lost my life through hypothermia, had it not been for our dog, Rebel, a Heinz 57 kind of dog, his name described him very well, and this made him all the more lovable and one of the family. We were spending another very cold night in our caravette, on a mobile home site at Zouch, Hathern in Leicestershire, County Caravan Park, when Clem was suddenly alerted by Rebel on the bed pawing at his face, at this time we were in a caravette conversion from its previous use as an ambulance He sat up immediately, realizing that something was wrong. His first thought was to check on me, and he described later that I was not breathing and was like a slab of ice. He thought I was dead. Panic took hold of him; he had faced nothing like it before, but he remembered reading somewhere that if a person is very cold the circulation should be restored by slowly warming the body and gently bringing life back into it. He wrapped me in a woollen blanket and set about massaging me back to life. Afterwards, when I was breathing normally again and out of danger, he attempted to light the cooker. Foiled again, the butane had frozen in the bottle. We later discovered we should have been using propane, which can withstand extreme temperatures. I have to thank Clem; once more he had been my saviour. He has been my rock; my guiding light throughout and I don't know what I would have done without him.

Moving into 44, Bidford Road on the 22nd January, 1986 was a disaster just waiting for us; the beginning of the end. The house was a tip, but then wasn't the council always teaching you a lesson that you had already learned? That did not perturb Clem in any way; he was still determined to ask his questions irrespective of whose cage he rattled. He met councillors of high standing, even the leader of the council, who lived not far away (but not in a tip of course!) He gained respect from them and was even invited to council meetings and forums. At one time he was invited onto the Broxtowe Residents Action Group (BRAG), but declined. What he saw was a power struggle within the organization; he didn't want to get involved in that. He also believed that it wouldn't be in our best interests. Why had they chosen him to become a spokesperson he would ask, believing that they didn't know enough about us? Word may get round about people and their lives, but that is not the same thing as knowing and understanding them, Clem always says that to know was to be pre-warned and, to be pre-warned is to be fore-armed. He was having none of it.

At this address, I was issued with my first social security number, which was to assist me to draw child benefit. It also sent my life into freefall, spiralling ever downward. On 16th January that same year I was awarded child benefit and received an order book to enable me to draw that benefit from the Department of Health and Social Security. My identity number on the Pension or Allowance book is before my very eyes: 91972659YM; issued to Mrs. Barbara Hall, 150 Andover Road, Bestwood Estate, in Nottingham. So I had recognition, and would receive child benefit for the first time, since a change in the law. Nothing wrong there, someone had their sums right, so why did it all go so drastically wrong from then right up to the present day? Were we to blame? To the best of our knowledge and belief, we have provided the information requested, but it's what happened to that information after we had supplied it that stands in question. We believe it has more to do with the Random Access Terminals (Electronic Link) where my problems manifested. Our tenancy at 44, Bidford Road had been established in the name of Hall. Nothing wrong there; everyone, from the council to our neighbours, knew who we were. No. Wrong again. Evidently there was a problem with my birth certificate and the pension that I was soon to draw, based on my husband's contributions. Wrong again, as I was to learn when I

176

reached the age of sixty-five in 1988 whilst we were living at that same address.

There were other numbers issued to me whilst I resided at that address: DHSS JE465994C DHSS 1098964, DHSS FY341308A, so at last I had a regular number that would provide me with my pension at my rightful retiring age. No. Wrong again, a further six numbers would be issued over the next few years, DHSS ZY077670D, which was easily recognised as a mistake and subsequently replaced with ZW077670D. This one is being used to the present day, but we have produced evidence to show conclusively that this number is not mine. That same number has been used by the Ministry of Pensions in different combinations of letters and numbers such as DHSS ZW465994D and JE077670C. The mind boggles as to what deception these departments are engaged in, and no wonder Clem refuses to have any dealings with any of them. Irrespective of the financial loss, he believes that one day they will be accountable, I am so glad that he fought them tooth and nail to hang on to my allowance books as the proof of what I have had to endure in order that these clerks save face for their incompetence, ineptitude and downright complacency, in order to escape detection.

So now after a long hard fight and struggle for identity, nationality and compensation for late pension I am enjoying life to the full, living it up, travelling, and taking holidays abroad – the very things I have yearned for, for many a decade. I can now marry my common-law husband of forty years, settle down to enjoy the rest of my life, with no further conflict to get in the way. No! Wrong again. It has still gone disastrously pear shaped. I am still being denied the truth and my day in court. That's the only kind of normal life that's on offer to me. I will gracefully decline and start the battle all over again until either they or I capitulate, or it ends with my demise. But the latter has no appeal for me whatsoever; battle on, is my war cry. I hope I am able to adequately portray the struggle and loss of freedom this has cost me. Nelson Mandela was incarcerated for twenty-seven years. Eighty-three years is three times as long, and the difference between his sentence and mine is that his was a confinement, whereas mine has been restriction. I would sooner have had his sentence, for it is over and done with, whereas mine continues until I get straight answers to straight questions. We will repeat and keep on repeating those questions until the answers match the law on the basis of its implementation and provision to deal with as set out in statute.

Many law firms have been involved in our search for the truth over the years and, to date, not one of them has been able to reach a satisfactory conclusion. Preliminary and basic enquiries into my case have always begun well, giving me fresh hope that a breakthrough would come. No. Wrong again. Sadly, when the story began to get complicated by red tape and officialdom, even the lawyers had to admit defeat. Many have thrown up their arms in desperation, even to suggesting that we accept the onus of responsibility in order that they strike it from the statute book. I say Never! Never!

It was also here at this address that I encountered one of the most frightening aspects of my life, Clem had been experiencing threats that the council were about to cave our door in to right a wrong of their making and, as Clem knew they were about to create another disastrous repair job as the like when they swept the chimney in February of that same year making it impossible for us to sit anywhere for fear of getting covered in soot truly I believe that these persons were not chimney sweeps) I hope they had a good laugh at our expense, this shows how very few friends we have made over the years in our quest for the truth.

Chapter 32   Fighting City Hall

Another solid brick wall proved to be impenetrable even though Clem tried all ways and means to shake its foundations. It was called City Hall, the home of the Council, brought into existence to take charge of all official and municipal affairs, whilst also bearing responsibility for the welfare and propriety of its citizens. The first part may be correct, but I would seriously doubt the accuracy of the latter part of that sentence. The real fight with the council was shortly after our door was smashed down during Nicholas Ridley's Right to Buy policy. We had decided to opt out as council tenants with all their rigor of what you could and could not do. Purchasing the house seemed at the time to be a good idea, but sadly, in reality, it was not. There were certain others who were prepared to go to extraordinary lengths to ensure that this did not happen.

Clem had become a thorn in the side of the council with his persistent delving into my past, and they found no way of stemming his questions relating to my birth certificate. In short, he had become a nuisance. He had also taken more than a passing interest in law, reading avidly into the early hours of the morning, and he soon became quite proficient. It was almost like second nature to him, as he had the ability to answer a question with another question, and he was so perspicacious that it irritated officialdom. They accordingly adopted a disdainful attitude and their rudeness sometimes bordered on belligerence; doors became locked and bolted to keep him out, and he also received the silent treatment. This procedure was intended to wear him down; during their meetings behind closed doors, staffs were ordered not to engage in conversation with him, and not to assist him in any way.

It was all wasted on Clem and didn't perturb him at all, as he always said he was a man with a mission, on an errand of mercy, for his own sake as well as mine. There would be no giving up until the job was finished and only he would decide when that was to be. No stone would lie unturned until he had fulfilled his quest. I never imagined it would take so long, not that I am complaining or ungrateful in any way – just the opposite in fact, and I couldn't be more proud of him than I am right now – I just wish that I could find the right words to tell him so. He openly admitted to me that he had no idea where to begin, as there were so many twists and turns to this story of mine and it must have taken a great deal of mental strength for him to keep track of developments. As Clem has said to me more than once, it's no good just keeping up with these people, you have to be at least two steps ahead of them all the time. I have been told by some officials that I am sucking eggs, whatever that is supposed to mean. Do they think because I am a grandmother I need teaching… or do they want me to teach them?

Sometimes, Clem would find himself really up against it, and there were days when we both felt discouraged. My despondency would show in my face and he would say, 'Don't worry love, I am not giving up. I will never abandon your cause, it is too important,' and he would squeeze my hand, renewing his promise to do everything in his power to uncover the truth, to find out the facts that would give me the peace of mind I so desperately craved after years and years of uncertainty and grief.

Each morning Clem would set off with his briefcase to do battle with officialdom. Clean shaven and dressed smartly, he attracted a fair amount of attention and, being intrigued by his manner, people would sidle up to him and ask if he were a lawyer. His reply was always that he was a McKenzie man. Most had no idea what a McKenzie man was, but those who did felt a few shock waves – enough to unnerve them, anyway. Clem was not bothered; to him it was all a game, like Blind

Man's Bluff, a load of codswallop. Another phrase he favoured was, 'Keep an ace or two; you never know when you might need them. Never ever be prepared to reveal all, but keep them guessing, it will do no harm, and that way you can always enter into contention on all aspects of your life.' It is true that Clem usually does have a trick or two up his sleeve.

I never for one moment thought it would take half of my lifetime to resolve a matter of deception that should never have occurred in the first place. When this matter is finally resolved (and it must be resolved in order for my life to have any meaning), I can say to all those who have become involved in this long-running saga, I told you so; I was not lying. The turn of events has fragmented my life, but the secrecy surrounding it all has been devastating. There are times when it all seems irreparable, and beyond hope, but if we give up now, all Clem's efforts will have been pointless, so we soldier on and try to keep faith when the outlook is bleak.

Every time we asked for information about my earlier years, those we questioned went into secrecy mode. We were repeatedly given the stock replies, 'We are not at liberty to say'; 'We are bound by departmental procedures'; 'The matter is closed'; 'Get your solicitor to write in on your behalf'. Some of their replies were absolutely ludicrous to say the least, but there was nothing we could do about it, as this was the way the system was being run. We soon became acclimatized to all the garbage being thrown our way, and they were certainly past masters in the art of deception, hiding away behind their air of respectability and appearance of doing good works for the benefit of all. Was any of it for my good though? I would suggest not; they were certainly biding their time, dragging their heels, making me wait months for a reply. 'There are others in the queue before you,' was another well worn put-down that they came out with. Operating at a snail's pace as they did, you wonder how any work within those departments was ever concluded. However long it takes, though, I must continue until I can say my life is in order to my own satisfaction and no one else's. There is still uncertainty ahead, and nowhere to hide even if I wanted to, but I have to see it through to the end, whatever the outcome.

I still cannot comprehend why Henry Hall should have been a constant visitor to a travelling gypsy family when I was a child. Did he visit bearing money and, expensive gifts out of the goodness of his heart? Is that really likely? I have often thought it a possibility that I could be the unrecognized offspring of some landed gentry. There has been too much importance attached to concealing the truth of my origins and protecting me from prosecution when I have broken the law, may I add deliberately and willingly in what I admit may have been a misguided attempt to secure a court appearance, in the hope of bringing the difficulties about my identity under the spotlight.

There were many attempts to remove our son from our care, continued threats to incarcerate him by the Social Services and the Education Authorities, all of which had a telling effect on our lives – and still these official bodies would not come out into the open and say what was concerning them about us as a family.

A lot of water has passed under the bridge and the simple life is all I want now; to find out the truth and then to be left alone in old age with my memories, good or bad.

There has been much speculation as to what actually happened or why, and we should not be interrogated about what could or might have happened. This is a straight forward issue concerning a falsified document for which there is no explanation or verification. Not just any document, but MY birth certificate. Sometimes overlooked is the fact that I am the innocent in all this – the victim of circumstances beyond my control, but whilst we remain up against the closed ranks of this country's bureaucracy, I will remain the nameless one with no proof of identity, still seeking co-operation from the authorities.

The Registration of the Individual Act states quite clearly that any Registrar acting within his office calls upon a person to register a birth whether it be stillborn or otherwise, in accordance with the law. If that person fails to do so, then they are summoned before the court to explain their actions. I now pose this question to the City Council of the particular Registration District holding the record of my birth: how and why was my birth falsely registered right under their very noses? Who had knowledge of the truth, and why was it concealed? Those responsible for this treacherous act have ruined my life, and until these questions are honestly answered, I will never be at peace, so will they please stop telling me that the matter is closed. They know, as well as I, that it most certainly is not and never will be until I get straight answers to my questions, to which I am entitled as a matter of law. This has had grave consequences and knock-on effects throughout my immediate family and their families, who also have fabricated details on certain documents. It is time this came to an end – no more excuses please, no more procrastination! The time is now.

Chapter 33   Bigamy

One definition of bigamy is 'a criminal offence committed when someone still legally married marries someone else.' The Oxford English Dictionary defines it similarly, 'the crime of marrying when one is lawfully married to another person.' Oscar Wilde famously joked that bigamy was one wife too many and in his view, monogamy was the same thing!

At the turn of the twentieth century, divorce was still hard to obtain and bigamy, though illegal, was quite prevalent and anyone convicted found themselves paying the price with a stretch of hard labour in the harsh prison conditions of the day. Today it is relatively rare, and the official figures a century later reveal that out of seventeen prosecutions in England and Wales in the year 2000, twelve were convicted and only four were imprisoned. Those detained at Her Majesty's Pleasure served an average sentence of five months for their sins.

I committed bigamy when I married Clem. Oh yes, I was fully aware that my marriage to George Worrall was still in force – there had been no divorce. Divorce, I was told by solicitors trying to help me, was not possible. Why not? Well, to qualify for divorce, you have first of all to be married. Wasn't I married to George Worrall, then? Apparently, not in the eyes of the law. Because of the false details on my birth certificate, my marriage was not legally recognized. Fine. No obstacle stood in my way then. I was legally a spinster and free to marry Clem, who had been married but was now legally, divorced. Wrong again!

Thus I found myself in a Catch 22 situation. I could not divorce George because I was not legally married to him and yet if I married Clem I would be committing a criminal act. I believed that one way out of this mess was to have the marriage annulled; make a fresh start. Wrong yet again. Annulment must be applied for within three years of the date of the marriage. Missed it by more than twenty years! There seemed to be no solution to my iniquitous situation and all I wanted was to be recognized as Clem's legal wife. After twenty-four years of living, eating and sleeping with this man, I wanted to be able to say he's my husband; I never asked for more than to be his happy wife.

I rose early on the morning of 10th May, 1991. Clem had told me that he was taking me over to Nottingham on that day but he wouldn't say where or why. He has always been full of surprises, and this would be no different to any other outing; he always kept one guessing but he never let on. He dropped me off at my daughter's and then journeyed into town. I learned later that he had purchased another birth certificate for Barbara Shaw, and then asked to see the registrar, whereby he was invited in to the registrar's office and told to be seated.

"Hello Mr. Clements! How can I help you today?" His manner was always impeccable. Whenever I have been there with Clem during his quest for information, he has always been the same. And this occasion was apparently no different. Clem hated it and called it the clinical approach; he could never ruffle his feathers. But he had done just once, about nine months previously, when a newspaper article had circulated on Friday 31st August, 1990, with the headline BIRTH CERTIFICATE MIX UP HOLDS UP MARRIAGE FOR OVER TWENTY YEARS. This was in an issue of the County Press, on the Isle of Wight, and was the first publicity ever to cause concern, not only to people who knew us, but also in government circles. It resulted in a visit by officials to the registry office in Shakespeare Street, Nottingham.

When Clem next went there, he was informed that he was barred from the premises. Not a problem for Clem; he would just phone instead. The ban was lifted shortly afterwards;

it constituted an infringement of his rights as it was a public building, open to all.

We had been stranded on the Isle of Wight, because having recently returned from the Republic of Ireland, Clem's native land; we were then confronted with iron grills on all the windows, bars on the doors, and padlocks everywhere. We had spent a memorable three week holiday in Ireland, so enjoyable that we would probably have stayed longer, but unfortunately our son had to face the courts for motoring offences. This is the kind of thing that crops up when you least expect it. We had chosen not to produce our documents to the Police when stopped, as we wanted the law to take its course. The aggravation we were being subjected to was too big a price to pay; the estate where we lived became known as Alcatraz. There were five exits off the estate, but it was known which one you were leaving from.

Clem and our son were later offered free pardons for their convictions for motoring offences that turned out to be nothing more than figments of certain persons' imagination. However, Clem would not hear of it.

"Let the convictions stand, that will guarantee we will be left in peace for a while," he insisted. But this had only come about by Clem's knowledge of the law. On one occasion he appeared in court to answer charges brought by the Nottinghamshire Constabulary, and offered a no-plea to the charges read out to him. Complete silence fell over the court room and utter confusion reigned as the Bench struggled to deal with it. Clem had fathomed out how the law worked, but the magistrates that day were completely out of their depth.

This plea was not known by many persons and, to Clem's knowledge, had only been given on one other occasion. That also occurred in a Nottingham court, and the woman in that case was sentenced, rightly or wrongly, to seven days in prison;

all a bit like the Fifth Amendment. Clem's appearance in court to face the charges brought against him and our son was a brilliant legal victory that could not have come at a better time for us.

All this harassment came about shortly after the door of our home was annihilated by an officer armed with a sledge hammer. A frightening situation, when you consider that this normally only happens when real emergencies arise, or in siege circumstances where someone is being held hostage against their will (I suppose in some ways, I could describe myself as such until I obtain an identity and passport). There are also situations where someone is in possession of drugs or explosives, but none of these were ever in our home. So what justification could there be for smashing our door down on the evening of Friday the 23rd October 1987? It was exactly twenty years and one week since Clem and I had met and fallen in love. There's that twenty-three again; the number that has dominated my life since the day I was born.

We had been warned that this would happen to us if we didn't allow the council into the property to rectify a fault which, incidentally, they themselves had created. They had been into the property some months before, and their workmen had made a hasty retreat away from the property after rendering the place uninhabitable. Clem decided he didn't want a repeat performance, and as a result we had to do without any kind of heating or hot water for the next ten months. It is obvious to anyone reading this account, that we were victims of our own circumstances, but equally clear was the disturbing fact that someone was out to deal us a bad hand and meant to do us real harm.

We weren't able to stave off the threats or the subsequent actions. It was a very worrying time for us; we found it all difficult to comprehend and lived in fear of what would happen next. Drastic though it may sound, that was the reason why Clem decided on his course of confrontation ? by persuading me into a bigamous marriage with him. This would bring about notoriety through scandal and sensationalism, which it most certainly did. It started the tongues wagging and created a far-reaching effect. It caught the officials with their pants down, which Clem had predicted, and we had now secured a defence regarding our bigamous marriage.

All this stemmed from my identity crisis, of course. We knew we were doing wrong, as we are both great respecters of honesty and truth, but who in this case cast the first stone? Should I have rolled over at the command of those who would be my masters, to enable them to put their house in order? I had always rolled over and played dead in all confrontational situations, giving in too easily and never standing my ground, even when I knew I was in the right. That is why everyone took an unfair advantage of me, I was easy pickings. But Clem has now shown me the other side of the coin. He has always stressed, 'never be too hasty; bide your time; your turn will come; the day will arrive when you will rejoice.' What he forgot to mention though, was how long it would be before this rejoicing would come about and I don't believe even he thought it would take four decades and then some!

So here I was, a bigamist, having married Clem with the full knowledge that my husband was still alive. I was also fully aware that bigamy and perjury would incur a custodial sentence upon us both. Clem constantly reassured me that if he had his sums right and he had correctly understood what he had read in the law books; there would be no charges to face. The most staggering thing was that Clem was absolutely right.

Weeks later, when neither of us had been arrested, we put forward our plans for a second bigamous marriage, and a third if necessary! The world was our oyster; we had at long last managed to attract attention to our plight.

Chapter 34   Fear And Secrecy

These two emotions go hand in hand. When you have shameful secrets, there is also the added burden of fear. Fear that your secrets may become known. You find yourself afraid to trust anyone and that is the one thing that you are really desperate to do - to confide in someone, to share the overwhelming, soul-destroying guilt that eventually takes over your life to the extent that you fear for your sanity. Since I was taken by the Halls, I have learnt that what happened to me was not only wrong, but it was also deliberate. I bear them no grudge; they were probably forced to keep the secret of my birth in the same way that others have been prevented from telling me the truth about whom my biological father was. The possibility of my ever finding out is very slim. The question I am asked is, do I have the right to know? In the light of the emotional turmoil I have had to endure, I can only say that I believe everyone who finds themselves in similar circumstances should be enabled to find out the truth. Then they will not be forced to grow into old age the way I have had to, still trying to discover why my life is still shrouded in secrecy, which creates fear not only for me, but also for other members of my family.

All my trials and tribulations began on the day I was kidnapped. I use the word kidnapped in its legal context. If these two persons Robert Mark Hall and Violet Hall were not my biological parents and had no legitimate right to take me from a secure environment, then there is no other way that the incident can be described, other than as a kidnapping. From the moment I was taken away, fear and secrecy was my everyday companion. All the dodging and hiding we were doing all over the country; stealing, begging and whatever it took to survive, became an everyday burden for me that has been hard at times to even think about. It is for Clem's sake and our son, and also the generations I shall leave behind, that I have to know the truth. If that is not possible, then my wish is that someone will continue with the research after Clem and I are too old to do so, in an effort to solve this mystery that has haunted every fibre of our beings.

On one occasion we started to get too close to the truth for comfort, and the situation became ugly. There were threats thrown our way, and we were warned repeatedly to back off. This in itself was quite disconcerting especially when combined with the previous threats and warnings that we had encountered. However, we decided to forge ahead. There had been several threats to remove our son, Darran from our care, mainly because of his loss of schooling through illness, but there were other reasons for his lack of attendance at school. The other children and teachers constantly picked on him, subjecting him to mental and emotional bullying and he had to run the gauntlet many, many times.

When he was fourteen years of age we were informed by the school that they were considering sending Darran to a special needs school. This was a cruel assertion and totally wrong for a boy of his character. Admittedly, he was a quite reserved boy who hated school because of what it was making him into, and I suppose he would have inherited some of this from my own background. But could it also be another way of getting us to move on, so that we would not then keep asking the awkward questions that they had been ordered not to answer?

At this time, Darran was a pupil at the Wilsthorpe Road School in Long Eaton, Nottingham, having moved school from Roper Lower, where again he had not been allowed to fit in. There was one occasion there when he had been forced to play football whilst he had a broken toe, which he had sustained when a street railing fell on him. He eventually received two hundred and fifty pounds compensation. One day, during the time of his attendance at the Wilsthorpe School, we had a visit from a Mr. Collins from the Derbyshire Education Authority. He asked our permission to give Darran an aptitude test, and we immediately agreed, knowing that he would come through with flying colours, which he did. The test was given by Mrs. Whitaker and Mrs. Horne who was the School Attendance and Welfare officer was present throughout the test. When it was over, we were approached by Mrs. Horne who said, "Don't look so glum. Darran is a highly intelligent boy; he is just lacking in certain academic learning. We will place him in Mrs. Thomas's class until he catches up and then he will be introduced back into the mainstream schooling."

Several weeks later when we asked him how he was doing in his new class, he replied that he was still in the same class, still being abused by the teachers and getting involved in fights every night on his way home from school. He was bloodied every time he returned from school, but he wouldn't let us intervene for fear of exacerbating the situation, and told us that as long as it was one to one, he could deal with it. Eventually, we could see that it was getting him down, and though he liked school and had gained the support of some pupils who had been bullied in the same way, we decided to pull him out of school permanently when he was fourteen years and three months of age. Darran received no more State Education from then on. Clem wrote a note to the Headmaster explaining our actions but, true to form, we never heard another word on the subject from either the school or the Board. The letter went something like this Dear sir, after careful deliberation we have decided being the parents of Darran a pupil in your school to have him taught Education Otherwise (EO) we therefore request you to remove his name from your register according to the Education Act 1944.

It had been our intention to move from King Street in Long Eaton for some time on advice from a reliable source who told us that the Education Authority's intention was to have Darran incarcerated until he was nineteen. We were living in fear from day to day, not only because of the threats regarding Darran, but also over loss of benefits and possessions, not to mention our respectability.

We knew that if we could get away from there, we would enjoy a respite for a few months until it all flared up again and of course we knew it would. The person who informed us became a close friend and said she would gladly take Darran to her home. She was concerned that he wasn't being given the chance that he deserved. During a conversation with Clem she told him that her own mother had deserted her and her father when she was just ten years old and, now her mother was old and had contacted her, wanting to come back into her life. She said adamantly that this was not going to happen after all the bitterness of her mother's years of absence.

Clem said, "You know, if you do not give her the chance to explain you may regret it for the rest of your days, but of course the decision is yours."

A few weeks later she saw us in the street and thanked Clem for his advice. She was over the moon because she and her mother were at last reconciled and she realised that it was what she had truly wanted all along, but had denied herself the chance to put things right.

Previous to withdrawing Darran from school, Clem had gone into the main library on Angel Row in Nottingham to research Education law and found himself a copy of the Education Act 1944 (he still has this copy to the present day), and passed this information on to many parents who were under threat of losing their children for no apparent reason. Under this act, at least 90,000 children up and down the country are being taught at home.

My greatest fear now is that if I don't solve this mystery in my lifetime, the fear and secrecy will continue unabated through generation after generation. My life has been given over to postulation, an assumption for future reasoning, Is this why in ecclesiastical terms my marriage was set aside in order to make my 'bigamous' marriages to Clem legal, thereby avoiding prosecution and ending this lifelong penance I am having to serve for wanting to know who I am?

Our son is curious about his grandparents on his father's side; this is natural, and maybe others within the family are also enquiring about their forebears. Well, the more the merrier, probably if enough of us ask the same questions, this could bring some pressure to bear on those who hold the answers. Otherwise, the records regarding my origins are being withheld until the year 2026. This will be far too late to bring any happiness into my life. I just ask that the birth records of the little girl known as Barbara Hall can be revealed and if there are none, then I am truly a nobody. Or an alien.

I ask this question again: What is it that cannot be said about the circumstances of my birth and my life for fear of it being detrimental to National security? Surely there is no one alive today who could be adversely affected by revealing such information? Is there? We are told that there is a Freedom of Information Act that deals with such issues as these. That is just another travesty; there is neither freedom nor information available to me; no one wants to investigate the whys and wherefores of any part of my tragic life, not even to the point of offering me just a tiny bit of sympathy or understanding. There was, though, one letter that came close to expressing regret, and this was from the pension service, just before I received my 'pension', but that was deliberate, in an attempt to gloss over what that department had previously created to prevent me from drawing my State Retirement Pension for all those years.

But I have one consolation in all of this, which is that they did not break my spirit. I was made to struggle and fight all those years for my pension rights which had nothing whatsoever to do with the identity crisis. But what a result – I now have a pension and passport, and both are in different names! Sort that one out if you can; I rest my case.

Chapter 35   Henry Hall And Others

I never did get to the bottom of the mysterious visits by the celebrated bandleader, Henry Robert Hall and, certainly from an early age I bore the same surname and grew up as Barbara Hall, firm in the belief that this was my name. It has always struck me as odd that he shared a surname with Robert Mark Hall, my supposed father, and I have not reached any conclusion as to whether they were related in any way, or whether it was pure coincidence. Some people have asked me if I thought Henry Hall was my father. The truth is, I don't know. It is possible. Or he may have been acting as a go-between for a member of the aristocracy – a kind of father-by-proxy figure.

Henry Hall spent some time in the Nottingham area when I was a little girl, although this has consistently been denied by those who want to protect his good name and I can reassure them that it is not my intention to tarnish it in any way. After all, I bore the same surname, or so I believed, until to my horror I discovered it wasn't, leaving me in something of a dilemma. If I wasn't Barbara Hall and I couldn't be Barbara Shaw, who was I and what connection did I have with the name Hall and the visits by this world renowned celebrity?

I remember his visits vividly. How I would be scrubbed up and made to look pristine before his visits; the way he asked how I was, and the attention he gave to me. It seems almost purposeless to mention any of this now that I am not able to provide evidence of those visits, as I was when I traced the cottage in Willian, sixty-nine years after I was taken from there. My half sister would be able to tell me more, but she refuses without giving the reason why. Is it just another streak of her jealous, spiteful nature showing up again, or is there a more sinister reason for her silence? Still I will not waver, as I did not when I went to look for my childhood home at Roxley Cottages, in the village of Willian. That was such a special moment, and proved to the doubters as well as myself that I was not suffering from an over active imagination. Not only was it all real, but it was exactly as I had always described it – the village school close by that had only one classroom. I remembered it so well; these are my earliest and only memories of the time before I was taken away and there is now no doubt in my mind that I did not make it up.

One day I hope to have more to go on, when I discover further details about my background and those who make up the members of my family. We have documents of births, marriages and deaths, including my own supposed birth and marriage documents. Maybe with the help of a genealogist we could shed some light on whether my registration was falsified by an idle stroke of the pen or the more sinister explanation – that it was an intentional act of deception.

Henry Hall would have been in big demand in his heyday to provide entertainment at venues such as the large country mansions and hotels, some of which were in the north of the country. The Gleneagles is one that springs to mind. Things started to take off for him shortly after he was demobbed from the Royal Artillery as Gunner H. Hall. After considering his future he decided on a musical career, having previously discovered that his position as a trumpeter with the Salvation Army had been filled by someone else. During his time with the army he had written numerous marches for them, and throughout his career he wrote many tunes, one of which, Here's To The Next Time, became the famous signing off tune to his popular Henry Hall's Guest Night. He introduced Teddy Bear's Picnic and Rusty and Dusty to his children's spots, making the songs very popular with the youngsters. He would entertain the landed gentry, even royalty were guests at his musical events. He also wrote a book entitled Here's To The Next Time.

Violet's sister, Lily Goss, was also in demand to provide entertainment in her chosen capacity as a member of the oldest profession. I may be completely off course here, but I have often wondered whether I could possibly be the result of a liaison between Lily and a 'gentleman' – possibly a gentleman who could have faced ruin if the truth were ever to get out, and because of this she stole her sister's identity to record my birth. Just another scenario, but is it imagined, or real? My so-called birth certificate does name Violet as my mother, but something else I always knew was that Violet and Lily often swapped identities with each other. Violet once received a visit from the law, to explain how she had acquired a fur coat but omitted to pay for it. This story circulated for some time during my younger years. I do not know the outcome, but their brother Billy also used many aliases which included Billy Graham. He also used the name Billy Price, the surname of the woman he lived with for many years, as well as his own name William (Billy) Goss.

I was regularly dumped on the doorstep of Arthur and Martha Graham with whom I would stay in Sheffield for weeks on end before the Halls collected me. I would have been living in Dalton Brook at that time, and it was always a case of, "Get up and get your things, we're taking you to Arthur and Martha's." I never had any choice in the matter. The Grahams had a daughter called Hilda, slightly younger than myself. The one strange thing I remember is that I had to share the bed with them. Where Hilda slept and, why I didn't share her bedroom would take some explaining, and I find it all so weird… could I have been born to be abused? No wonder my life is so topsy-turvy.

Can I think of anything good to say about my childhood that would soothe away so many bad memories? I search my mind and, one thing is uppermost. They, my so-called parents, have taken this secret to their grave, now there is only my half-sister Lily who could give me some indication of why it all took place. But alas, that will never happen now as she is too old, as well as unwilling, to reveal anything. When we used to meet with her on friendlier terms, she could be quite pleasant and eager to share the story with Clem. The pity is, we were not doing any research at that time, and for that reason, nothing was ever recorded for us to refer back to. Our real problems began when it became apparent that I was not going to be able to claim my pension. There had been a pension forecast sent to my husband, George, notifying him of the joint pension we were to receive. He must have notified them that I was no longer his spouse, and I should then have received a separate forecast in my own name. This did not happen. It was only then that I realised what a dire mess I was in.

Ironically, Robert Hall's words ring in my ears, when he mysteriously said to me, "Remember, you will never get a pension in that name..." He gave away no clue as to what he meant by such a remark. What did he know that he dared not tell me that might have eased the burden of what I have since had to bear? Years later, has the light dawned, is this what he meant?

Henry Hall had been a civil servant with the Ministry of Pensions and I quote from his book, 'I was demobbed in February 1919 only to find, like hundreds of thousands of others, that my pre-war world no longer offered me anything I wanted.' He decided not to return to the Salvation Army but did return to being a civil servant as a temporary clerk, in the Ministry of Pensions in the Wallace Collection in Manchester Square. As an employee of that department, he would certainly be qualified to know the position regarding such situations.

Another interesting fact is that he had also at one time worked as a page boy to Lord Bradbury. This could possibly tie in with the mysterious visits he paid me, always with some gift and a bundle of money for my mother. I don't ever remember seeing my father around when these visits took place; my half-sister was always there, but no attention was ever given to her and she was always at her most spiteful after he had gone. These explanations seem quite feasible and very obvious to me but, strangely, they have always been dismissed as fantasy or wishful thinking on my part, and then the shutters of silence have fallen once more, preventing me from going any further.

One solicitor, on the Isle of Wight, who was representing us through the Legal Aid Board, made a very strange observation. His comment may have been made to disguise the fact that he was getting nowhere, but in a letter which said a lot but told us nothing, he wrote that a name, after all, was just a label. I don't think I would get away with putting the coffee label on the tea caddy or vice versa!

We strongly resented his 'let sleeping dogs lie' attitude, and chose not to visit the so-called top solicitors in Ryde again. We were constantly knocking our heads against brick walls trying to find answers from those who should have been able to find the answers. No information was ever shared with us, but we feel sure that certain aspects were revealed to the solicitors that we engaged at the expense of the state and, after our initial interview, the reception on our subsequent visits to these solicitors cooled dramatically, which delivered us back to nowhere. This is the whole sorry tale... no one is revealing anything; we are met with, 'you have been here before' or some such idiotic excuse. Clem says if you want to wear someone down, keep turning up on their doorstep – it does wonders for the spirit!

## Chapter 36					Isolated And Alienated

Although my marriage to George Worrall had not been satisfactory for some time, our family life carried on in a more or less normal fashion and, to the outside world at least, we were no different from other families of the age. I had for some time, experienced a kind of inner nagging, a desire to try to solve some of the puzzling aspects of my past. For instance, why was I suddenly taken from a perfectly good and loving home and bundled away with gypsies as a child? What was said by the registrar to Robert that I was not allowed to hear, just prior to my marriage in 1945? I wanted to try and find some answers to these questions and I began by going to get a copy of my birth certificate, naively supposing that this would give me the answers. Not so. It only threw up many more questions. But it was the beginning of another very depressing and lonely period for me.

Realizing that my birth records were wrong, that I had no idea who I really was and that even my marriage was a sham, brought back all those emotions from my childhood, when I was treated as a social outcast. I could not talk to my husband about it. I did try to but he was unconcerned with any of the implications and simply shrugged it off and refused to discuss it, saying 'Don't start on that again!' I had no confidante, nowhere to go and no one to help me. I felt desolate and desperately worried and it was one of the worst times in my life.

No one can doubt that this had a devastating effect on my life. From here on I was very lonely, even with my immediate family, and everyday family life had no meaning for me any more. I was becoming more and more isolated and alienated to the point of screaming and I knew I dare not do that, remembering that my so-called mother used to have many screaming fits. I remember how I would tell Robert I was going to call an ambulance, when he would panic and beg me not to, as she would be put in the 'Loony Bin'. After a while she did calm down and I learned later that she thought at such times someone was trying to enter her body. I thought that kind of thing only happened while you were asleep, but she was always wide awake when it happened. I have always said that I was from a strange breed; and so I ask myself do I really want to know the whole truth? There may be more to this than meets the eye; I remember Robert once telling me that his mother died in a mental institution.

What did I make of all this at the time? Not a lot. I wish I had been a more persistent person, and then I would have found the answers to my ever questioning mind. No single answer would suffice at this stage, but I am gradually getting there, and with Clem's patient counselling we are, little by little, piecing together my fragmented life. Not for a single moment throughout my life with Clem have I had any doubts about his honesty and integrity. I know things haven't been easy for him and in some ways he has probably suffered more than I. His world has been one of denial. Unable to marry me legally until he knows who I am, and that I am free to do so; bigamous marriages are okay, but if they don't get the desired results, they're not worth the paper they are written on.

Let's meditate for a while on what I really have for my future, so that I can look back, not in anger to proclaim that I put the world to rights, but because I genuinely believe that I have changed the course of history, that certain legislation is now being implemented to prevent future generations suffering the same fate that we have. We will go on doing what we do best, irrespective of whose cages we rattle. Everyone has the right to know their origins and biological parentage, and to deprive them of such information is an offence in law. There is also the moral aspect, and that could present an even stronger challenge than the legal one.

The burning question I ask of the legal profession is this: Why has my case taken so much from the legal purse (to the tune of two hundred thousand pounds), and who are these charlatans who have masqueraded as professionals to obtain money from their clients under false pretences? One day we shall name them all. Clem did warn me what they were all about, remarking that no politician or solicitor should take on a case unless they were qualified to see it through to a satisfactory conclusion. He is able to expose them for what they are worth. Though he is a determined man and has taken all my problems very seriously, he also has a robust sense of humour and I remember him saying to me one day, "Imagine you are visiting a solicitor and then you are called into his office, can you picture a rhinoceros sitting there?"

"Why?" I asked naively. "What do you mean?"

"Because there is no difference between them, they are both short sighted, both thick skinned, but always ready to charge." No wonder Clem sometimes had me in stitches; his wit was rarely matched when in a buoyant mood. But he was deadly serious on the occasion when he deliberately set out to prove that these so called professionals had no genuine interest in their clients' problems whatsoever. Over a period of two weeks he visited thirty legal firms, and not one of them guessed what had happened until it was too late. He stated his case to the first one, which was hastily accepted and the green legal aid forms duly appeared and were then signed for the solicitor to complete one and a half hours work on his case. He then left the office, and repeated this little exercise thirty times. Clem was determined to show that there was little or no work done on his behalf. Then he waited.

"What goes around comes around you, will see," he told me.

Towards the end of the two weeks Clem made an appointment with another firm of solicitors, but when he arrived at their offices, he was told he didn't have an appointment. Clem then produced his appointment slip, whereupon the receptionist informed him that the Legal Aid Board had cancelled any further assistance in view of what he had done. Unfortunately, the solicitors had all committed the cardinal sin of ignoring their own small print by not asking (as stated on the green form), 'Have you had assistance in the past three months for matters you have discussed with me today?' Clem replied that it was never asked; if it had been he wouldn't have proceeded because that would have been criminal deception. Clem was not out to break the law, merely to prove a point – you can fool some of the people some of the time, but you cannot fool all of the people all of the time. What Clem did may sound extreme, but he showed that he was prepared to stand and fight bare knuckle if necessary, and I was truly proud of my man.

To every problem there must be a root cause, and something or somebody caused my birth to be falsely registered. Someone was responsible for the action that has resulted in the deprivation I have been forced to suffer over the years, even though it is belligerently denied by the council and registry office. I believe that it could have been the Lord Chancellor when I was made a Ward in Chancery. This notion has been dismissed by the authorities as utter poppycock, but it might explain the visits by Henry Hall, the handing over of money to Violet and the presents and attention paid to me. I also think it possible that I was some VIP's love child, and that is why I was placed with foster parents until I was so cruelly taken from their loving care. It is the only possible reason I can find for my predicament and why the authorities have consistently refused to budge.

Ordinary people may not know what a Ward in Chancery is; it is more commonly referred to as a Ward of Court, and anyone interfering with such an order does so at their peril. The Lord Chancellor has jurisdiction for all matters relating to the Ward from the day of the order, and would therefore be responsible for all matters relating to me, had I been made a Ward of Court. He would decide how much money was to be allocated for my upbringing and education, and where it was to be; my clothes and pocket money, etc would be provided for at his discretion, even when and where I could be taken on holiday. So could this be an explanation for those regular visits by the renowned Henry Hall? After all, we know he had once been a Civil Servant and received the MBE and CBE.

Chapter 37   An Official Identity

What will it mean to me now that I have a name to call my very own after struggling for so many years of not knowing who I really was? From now on, I shall be known to family and friends and the world around me, as Jane Doe. The name, of my own choosing, has now been officially recognised and has the Home Office's stamp of approval. I thank them for their efforts to help me to achieve my one ambition in life – to have an official identity.   The work involved in sorting out the many complexities of my life must have been almost as difficult for them as it was for me to live with them.

I bear no one person any animosity or ill-will because of my iniquitous situation, but what I do say to those who have prevented me from uncovering the truth of my origins is this: may you never find yourselves in such a nefarious situation; those who have not lived and breathed the nightmare for their entire adult life can never understand what it has been like and I feel fortunate to have come through it with my sanity.

My life was never to be a normal one from the moment of my abduction/kidnap when I was almost five years of age. Not one person has been brought to book for taking me from the loving home where I was loved and cared for and placing me with a rough, travelling family who, although they claimed me as their own, made it clear from the beginning that they did not want me.   My fate was sealed that spring day, nearly eighty years ago when I just as unwillingly became one of their strange brood.

What my past means to me is endless sorrow and when I permit my mind to wander back to the beginning of it all, I still find it amazing that such things could have taken place and yet the truth about it all still remains hidden, all these years later. The only way I have been able to cope with my situation has been to try to uncover the past, to find out why I was taken, and why my birth certificate was falsified, leading to the difficulties and hardships I subsequently had to face.

I do not know the truth to this day and if anyone alive knows it, they are not telling why I was given so many false names, none of which I was entitled to use as my birthright. But I now have a name I can be officially identified by – Jane Doe – and at last I am able to start living as a normal person, with rights. For example, I have recently been able to obtain a digital hearing aid, which has opened up a whole new world – I can converse normally again, so beware to those who would utter unkind words, I can discern the softest whisper. I am to undergo surgery for cataracts – surely there will be no stopping me when both hearing and sight are fully restored?

Of one thing I am sure, my adorable husband will not want to exchange me for a newer model. If it were not for his initiative and intervention, his ingenuity and integrity, I would never have got this far. Clem is the love of my life and I thank him again from the very depths of my heart for his insight and understanding and for taking up the challenge on my behalf.

As I have mentioned in a previous chapter, one frequent visitor in my early life was none other than Henry Hall, a world renowned celebrity of his day. A thought has come to me – could this be an unsubstantiated reason for my being known as Barbara Hall, bearing in mind that my abductor/kidnapper was also a Hall, Robert Mark? But the question on my lips has always been… why would a person of such standing as Henry Hall, a CBE as well as an MBE, come calling on a young gypsy girl, bestowing her with the title of 'Lady Barbara'? I am not suggesting anything relating to his frequent visits nor speculating on any possible connections with Robert or Violet Hall or myself, other than the fact that it does pose more questions than can, apparently, be answered.

I am more content now that I have an official identity, albeit one that has nothing to do with the name on my contrived birth certificate. I have the freedom to leave these shores and return without too much notice, providing that the duration of any visit abroad does not extend beyond thirty days – this is because of the social benefits I receive. So when I say 'freedom', it is with tongue in cheek; in fact, I am still restricted by the red tape that the Nottingham South MP, Alan Simpson referred to in 1994 as practically strangling me.

My life has always been bound by restrictions, the like of which have surely not been imposed upon any other blameless and innocent person such as myself. I am confident in my belief that something in my past has been and is still being concealed, and not just from myself and my family, but from the general public. So what is this secret that is too detrimental and damaging to be revealed, even to me now in my eighties?

If I could have this favour granted to me by some faceless individual currently lining the corridor of power, I swear I wouldn't breathe a word to another living soul... in your dreams! I would shout it from the rooftops and I'd be there at the world's biggest press conference to ensure that it became one of the greatest exposé of our age. How I have longed to explode with a tirade, uttering words the like of which have never escaped my lips; to strike back with new found confidence at the establishment that has tormented me with secrecy and conspiracy from day one, when I set out to discover the truth, and to find my lost (or stolen?) identity.

For the record, I would not change one minute of the last forty years of my life spent with Clem, but what of the life that should have been mine by law? There is no doubting that our lives would have taken a different course if we had been given truthful answers to our questions from the outset. For one thing, we would have been able to marry legally and there would have been no anxiety over our son's legitimacy. The next issue that springs to mind is money and the security it provides – had my pension rights been recognised, Clem and I could have been enjoying our retirement in our own little home somewhere, instead of having to rely on various lets, some of which were barely fit to live in, and having no permanent postal address because we were never in a position to afford a place we could call our own. We survived all these hardships because we had each other, and we looked on the bright side and made the best of things.

To win one small battle – against the passport office – has given me renewed confidence and fresh hope. In a way, by being permitted to hold a passport in my adopted name of Jane Doe, I do feel reborn. I could have chosen any names I wished, including Bloggs or Smith, and Clem and I discussed all possibilities before deciding on Jane Doe. This is a name widely used in America for a dead, unknown person, often referred to as having 'no name, no face… alone and forgotten'. We both thought this quite befitting as there is no paper trail to my real being. Am I dead or alive? Nobody knows or, if they do, they are silent on the matter.

But our soul searching is beginning to pay dividends. At long last, my pension entitlement is being reviewed. I am not holding my breath, nor am I stupid enough to imagine for one moment that I will be given a cheque compensating me for pension entitlement that I have never been able to claim. But there may be something left in the pot for Jane Doe and if there is, however small, we will have won another round.

My own sense tells me that my first marriage in 1945 was never legal, but I can only go on proclaiming my innocence; the deception and subsequent mistaken identity was in no way due to my own actions. For me, for twenty-two years, ignorance was bliss. It was only when I took it upon myself to go to the registry office and ask for a copy of my birth certificate that the implications became apparent to me. Those who held high office at that time must bear the guilt; I have had to bear the shame. How do you think I felt, knowing that I had borne six illegitimate children? Do you wonder that I feared for my sanity?

To return to the subject of my pension, I do feel that I am entitled to receive all those years' back pension, but it is now a matter for the law and I will have to abide by their verdict. My argument is that I was led to believe that I would receive a state pension at retirement age, based on the marriage contribution deducted weekly from my husband's wage. He would have received the married couple's allowance as a joint payment. The fact that I left the marital home because of circumstances beyond my control should not incur such a penalty. I married in good faith, accepting my duties and, as far as I knew, abiding by the laws of the land. I realise that pleading ignorance very rarely has any effect but, in my case I feel that it was not just a question of my being ignorant of the facts, but more a case of having the wool pulled over my eyes.

It will be some time before I know whether the review will go in my favour or not. If it does not, what's new? If it finds in my favour, I will be better off financially, but I will still be Jane Doe who was once unknown and alone, but no longer hides her face in the shadows of shame.

Chapter 38   About Jane Doe

I suppose I am more qualified than most to talk about Jane Doe... after all I am Jane Doe with kind permission of the Home Office, after they capitulated by permitting me to bestow that name upon myself; a most befitting name for someone in such dire circumstances. Not because, as some suggest, that I am a dead body and quickly follow it up with the taunt that it cannot be my name... that I am alive... look I am here, living and breathing. There is another purpose behind the name Jane Doe other than being a dead body, which is that it refers to a litigant in person. With that name I can bring a case to court and be that litigant in person, and this is what I hope to do when I take my case into court for fourteen years' back pension rights and loss of retirement that pension would have given me. Now, at eighty-five, I am looking forward to my battle with the courts. I now know who I am... my passport states who I am... and would the Home Office issue such a document to a dead person? I hope this clarifies any doubts over the name Jane Doe; to some it will be an education in itself, and could even start a trend.

Now that I know who I am by virtue of my passport, a first in legal history in this country as far as we are aware, there are no bounds to what we can achieve if permitted to do so. I know who I am, but what I don't know is who I should have been, and possibly now is the right time to try yet again to find out. Prior to the issue of the passport to one Jane Doe, no solicitor would venture to take my case to court for me, having no true identity to officially establish who I was. This caused endless delays over my pension and benefits, until time limits were imposed – in my case three years. What we didn't know then was that there were no limitations that could be imposed until my official identity was confirmed. Now all this has changed; it has a new meaning and a real purpose. With my name of Jane Doe, I have been reborn, re-registered and have an admission that the establishment didn't know who to charge over my bigamous marriages.

Of course, I will have to exercise caution; now that I have a name to call my own, it could bring about a legal precedent, should I be so lucky. I chose to call myself Jane Doe in 1995 after consultation with a legal team who also drew up my will, which I duly signed in my legal name of Jane Doe. From there forward there should have been no doubts over my official identity, but we later discovered that this would not satisfy the requirements of those who had appointed themselves to be Power of Attorney over my affairs. Without my knowledge, they had decreed that I should not be permitted to be recognised by this name as it could cause embarrassment in certain society circles. So, having no official name from birth – apart from those forced upon me by deception, I was put in the unenviable position of never being able to state my case or seek legal advice to help me to do so.

I have come a long way from the days of trying to give an official name to our son. He has had to make do with pretend names as I have done, but that was apparently okay and in keeping with the rules of the registry office, who claim they have bent over backwards to assist with my dilemma. I would suggest try bending a little further... but I wouldn't want your backs to break! This new found freedom of speech which has been denied to me from birth and not made available to me until the age of eighty-three, will be like a whiplash cutting across those who dare to challenge me over my rights to the truth. I demand that they give an account of why I have been forced to accept a falsified birth record to be my own.

As the Reverend Ian Paisley, once put it, albeit in a different context, 'Never! Never! I am now on the pedestal for recognition by those who denied me, even among family members – those who were too pretentious to come out into the

211

open and discuss the effect this was having on their lives. No; Never. In my dreams again; too much resentment prevented this from happening, and guess what? We all make mistakes in our lives, but is there no honesty in the world any more? Was it pride and prejudice that stood in the way of being allowed to ask the simple question: explain to me how, did it all begin? I want to know, after all you are my mother... Was she? I don't know. Would she tell? Never!

I know where it all began for me as I journey back to that fateful day when, almost five years of age, I was taken away from the cottage where I felt safe and secure as a young child should be. Someone should be compelled to explain why I was taken away to start a new life with strangers, to adapt to their strange ways. I ask: did anyone spare a thought for me then? Does anyone spare a thought for me now? I tell you, I could count them on one hand, and another question I ask is this: is their concern genuine? I don't know. Do I care? I think not; mine has been a lonely battle with only the support of my beloved Clem. I could not have come through it without his help; we need more people in the world like him, then the treatment of people as second rate citizens would cease, and we would all be truly equal.

Where do I go from here? Well that's a tough one to answer. My life has been full of trauma and I have reached the crossroads of indecision. It is not easy for me to explain. I know we may have overstepped the legal mark from time to time, when we considered we had to do it to try to generate the oxygen of publicity needed to highlight our case on a wider plain, but this was to no avail, always turning out to be wishful thinking again. Is it now time for me to make an announcement – which I, Jane Doe, do declare, together with my husband Clem that I will abandon my four decades long quest for the truth as to who I am? If I do, (note that I say if) it will come as a great shock to the many who believed I would never capitulate, but it will be of my own volition and not a collapse under pressure from those at the controls.

I sometimes feel tired of it all, and that nothing further can be achieved now I have reached this time in my life. My story has aroused interest and suspicion the world over and there are those out there who simply will not let this enigma be put to rest. You know who you are, and you must watch your own backs as I have had to do, and be careful not to reveal your findings until you are sure you can do so in safety. This is a mystery the likes of which is unheard of, even in the realms of secrecy that exist within the fabric of this country's security. What has happened matters to me; I am after all, a human being and I do matter and, whatever the outcome, I want it known that I, Jane Doe, existed. I may never know the true identity of the woman beneath the surface but, as Jane Doe, my name will live on long after my demise. I am glad Clem chose that name for me… far better than Barbara Hall or Barbara Shaw. Who were they when they were alive? More to the point, were they ever alive?

Since that fateful morning when I discovered I was not Barbara Hall, and that there had never been a Barbara Hall officially, and as such could not hand over that name in marriage, I suddenly succumbed to the idea that I had been born an idiot. I felt like the idiot of all idiots. Why had I not suspected earlier that there was something tragically wrong in my life? Why had I always been so trusting of others? Part of the answer to that lies in the inherent need we all have of wanting to belong, so there are other, deeper issues here… emotional, psychological and spiritual. This goes way beyond a single entity, and the circumstances are too profound for the mind of one man to unravel. It must now be a matter for a court of competent jurisdiction to settle once and for all time; this mystery, going back eight decades has blighted the lives of too many.

Since the day I was kidnapped there has been concealment of my life and the circumstances relating to who had charge over me during the first four years of my life, and why. Surely this could only have been brought about by a Court Order? So, there should at least be a record worth searching for that could throw light on the earliest part of my life, which is a complete blank to me. It is wrong to deny that any such record exists; I believe it does and that it could lead to a lasting solution as to who I really am. One day, maybe... one day.

Throughout these chapters I have managed to come to terms with my life and the great deception, present from the beginning, which has grown with me – has indeed always been a part of me. This should never happen to any person, no matter what the real reason. To be forced to go through life from childhood to old age in ignorance of one's origins is an unspeakable burden to bear, and every person should have the right to ask and be told the truth about their ancestry whether or not it causes embarrassment to those who would prefer the facts to remain untold.

Most people reading this will be able to account for their lives and will have no doubt as to their identities. Unfortunately, there has been one big drawback to my quest for the truth... complacency, which I have encountered along the way from all walks of life, with the odd innuendo thrown in: you don't have to know who you are... as long as we know that's all that matters. I ask you to consider... is that right?

Chapter 39 The Mystery Of Missing Records

Understandably, I have at various times turned to a large number of professionals in the hope that they could use their expertise to help solve the mystery of my identity, or more correctly, non-identity. With Clem's help, I have consulted lawyers, doctors, MPs and other government ministers. Most have been more than willing to offer their assistance and support and matters have usually progressed pretty well. Up to a point, that is, and then we have been told that their enquiries can go no further. Invariably, the stage is reached when an answer from a government establishment comes back to the effect that a particular record 'does not exist', 'has been destroyed', 'cannot be found', or any other euphemism that can be used in order to slam the door on us and keep the true facts covered up.

I am deadly serious in my belief that there is something vital to my enquiries which is being deliberately withheld. This information, whatever it may be, is crucial in every aspect if I am ever to solve the mystery surrounding the whole of my life and other members of my family. They and I have a right to know who our forebears were; what walk of life they were conducting; whether they were tall, slim, fat, professionals, lawyers or politicians. Perhaps a pregnancy the wrong side of the blanket spelt ostracism and potential ruin for a member of the aristocracy, nobility or even a royal personage? I believe it is not beyond the realms of possibility.

Our endeavours will never cease; I have a right to know their origins, nationalities and how they interrelated with each other. With that background information I can then collate some idea of who my true forebears were and further proceed to discover why everything went so tragically wrong for me. I have to be told… no, I demand to be told the truth about why my official birth records are being denied to me until the year 2026 (recently amended from 2038).

It is true to say that for as long as I can remember, I have always carried doubts of who I really was and who my true parents were, but these doubts surfaced more predominately just after giving birth to my sixth child, Amanda, (Mandy). When she was but a few months old I was taken into hospital for a major operation and was persuaded to be permanently sterilized at the same time. There was very little discussion on the matter, but Miss Baker, the gynaecologist, at the Nottingham City Hospital strongly advised me to agree because of a serious risk to my life and health in the event of a further pregnancy. I gave it little thought and signed the papers for the operation to go ahead.

So, if I was permanently sterilized, what the hell went wrong? When I became pregnant in 1969 with Clem's child, no one believed me. Well, how could I have been, hospitals don't make those kinds of mistakes, do they? I was told repeatedly that I could not possibly be pregnant. Nevertheless, some mistake had occurred, and it was confirmed, after my third visit to the doctor's surgery, that I was indeed fourteen weeks pregnant. Then after this official confirmation, all panic let loose and there was a concerted effort to persuade me to terminate the pregnancy, which I thought was strange and unusual, but the reasons given were that my life and that of the unborn child could be at risk. I know I am harping back to events which occurred in my distant past now, but because of my circumstances this is what I do. I need answers to so many questions that every major event in my life seems to become a riddle in itself – my birth (the biggest riddle of them all); my education and working life; my marriage (now there's a conundrum: your marriage is not recognised by law, therefore you cannot be divorced, but if you marry someone else you will be committing bigamy); my retirement, etc.

If I could just find a few answers, then maybe, just maybe, I can get on with some semblance of a life before it's too late. The life has not gone out of me yet... I am still able to put up a good fight, or at least give as good as I get, and I am proud of what I am doing as many others are now relying on me to solve this iniquitous situation and my determination will see me through.

The identity problem should be easy enough to solve by means of Sir Alec Jeffrey's' pioneering technique of DNA genetic finger printing but who within the family would fall within that category? I do not know which bloodline I am from; it could be Shaw or it could be Hall, or of course it may be neither but I have the right to know. And that raises a further question – who will take on the government on my behalf to prove my identity once and for all? I am not talking here about the recent issue of a passport in my chosen name of Jane Doe. This is not the name I will carry to my grave. I still have all my faculties and the ability to fight and my dearest wish is that when I leave this world for another, I will hold all the relevant facts.

This strong fighting spirit within me is inspired by the support of Clem, who has often encouraged, and sometimes persuaded me, to break the law. Not with any criminal or wilful intent, but because it has sometimes been necessary in order for me to win my objective. We know full well that we are branded as habitual law breakers, liars and criminals along with many thousands more, but ours is with a purpose – to achieve a goal never before encountered, the like of which has seldom been heard of, let alone aired in a court of law.

Yet I feel that this will lead to a resolve of my present situation as to why the Home Office was able to grant me a passport in parallel identities of Shaw/Hall as well as nine differing NI numbers together with five NHS numbers. Could I have got it so terribly wrong or were there others involved? One day soon I hope to have the answers to these and many more questions that the establishment has so far refused point blank to answer. So now, in desperation, I shall take my leave for a while, and look at other opportunities which may bring about a resolve, either through the evidence that I hold myself or, more intriguingly, by revealing who I believe my biological father was from events in my past when I was compelled to go and live with my Auntie Lily. I feel more certain now than ever, that she was trying to reveal to me who my father was. Her words then meant nothing to me; I was just too young to understand. But... now things are different; there is a different meaning to her words, bringing more understanding and more purpose into everything I do.

I constantly search for the words I may have overlooked when my auntie and I sat by a warm fire, when she would talk to me as if I were her own child. I felt at ease, at home with her, and treasured the brief spells that I enjoyed in her care, dreading the return to my so-called mother, Violet. Life seemed to be always playing cruel tricks on me, could this be the reason it has manifested itself within my mind and given me the determination to prove that there is a profound mystery, not only by virtue of missing records but, also the secrecy surrounding those missing records? Missing records; missing answers; missing persons. There have been times when it was almost impossible to carry on but, I must, if only for the sake of our son, knowing how difficult it was to register his birth. In some ways this whole process is for his benefit and not mine. I have endured the knock-on affects throughout my life, and I feel it is up to me to see that he does not inherit any further doubt or secrecy relating to my mysterious birth and the disastrous consequences it has heaped upon me. I did not sow the seed and, I will not, I repeat will not reap the tainted harvest, the stigma that binds itself around all of us involved in this sorry saga.

When I have been required to answer specific questions, I have done so to the best of my knowledge and belief. If those questions and answers did not add up, be it not upon my head but on the heads of those responsible for all the deceit at the time of my birth. I can only ask again: how do I know that it was my birth or whether it (or I) was just a substitute? There are many irregularities and discrepancies in documents relating to other family members but, without their written permission, we are not permitted to ask any questions relating to them. We have been able to go so far inasmuch as we have been permitted to request copies of certain documentation – birth, marriage and death certificates following family history searches, but only after proving identity. There's that word again… identity. Most people can say it without any thought; but to me it conjures up a lifetime of not belonging, not counting. Until the missing records turn up, I will remain the "woman who never was".

So what could be the answer at this late stage in my life? I have already given an undertaking never to give up my quest for the truth; I am fully committed to seeing this through to the bitter end. Someone has to bow to pressure, but that someone will never be me. None of this preposterous business is of my making and the answer to one simple question would end all the uncertainty and speculation at a stroke: why my alleged birth certificate, a fabricated document endorsed by the District Registrar of the day, lay dormant for four decades, then suddenly emerged, causing me such devastating pain and anguish.

Someone was responsible; they may be dead now, but they would never have known or cared how it felt. I have continually searched my heart and mind in the hope that some little detail might lead towards a resolve. I have bent over backwards in my efforts to assist those who were ready to help, only to find that when they reached a sensitive point, they could hardly wait to show me the door. Until these people have a genuine desire to assist me in my endeavours, I shall not answer any more of their questions, I know that this will make me unpopular with the authorities, but as they already consider me to be a nuisance of the highest order, what have I to lose?

Chapter 40   Love Conquers All

All manner of obstacles can be scaled, providing we are prepared to give as well as receive the love we come to accept as a God given right. Most of us learn from our parents from a very early age, that love is a fundamental right. No one should be denied or deprived of love; throughout millennia love stories abound, many of them purely fictional. Nevertheless, these novels sell millions of copies. Because of our desire to be loved and wanted, we unconsciously enter the lives of the characters portrayed, which can sometimes help us to become better persons within ourselves. These love stories were an escape for me and I believe it was through reading them that I convinced myself that life was passing me by.

With the discovery that I was not who I had thought myself to be more than forty years on from my birth, my life suddenly became so hollow and meaningless; I realised my past had caught up with me and was over-taking me at a breathless pace. Thus began my endless days of searching for answers as to why now, at the threshold of middle age, I had made this discovery and, then the more sinister realisation that no one wanted to know about my torment. From that day I felt estranged from my family; it was an incredibly lonely feeling and I just went about my duties, not knowing what to expect in the future, but mentally preparing myself for trouble. It seemed inevitable.

Not for one day over the next three years did this nightmare leave my mind, nor did I find anyone to assuage my fears when I realised the enormity of it all and the possible future implications of this magnificent deception that I never even knew existed. I had no knowledge of my birth certificate details until long after my marriage, in fact it was nineteen years afterwards that I first had any inkling that something was wrong and it took me a further three years to summon the courage to delve deeper. I was therefore in no way responsible for the erroneous details, and it came as a terrible shock to me to find that I was not who I had always assumed I was. I had no reason to reproach myself but even so, the burden of guilt and shame was almost too much to bear at times.

On the morning of Monday 20th May 1991, I woke up with a feeling of apprehension and for a while I had serious reservations about going through with marrying Clem. Would, it be bigamous or not? Would we be arrested? Would our marriage be recognised legally? All these doubts went through my mind, but when I saw how much it meant to Clem I didn't have the heart to disappoint him. I had known nothing about it until ten days previously, when Clem drove me from Birmingham to Nottingham and obtained another copy of my alleged birth certificate, and then four days later we applied to the Registry Office for a marriage by special licence. There was some discussion between Clem and the registrar, but I managed to miss half of what was spoken about because my hearing aid had somehow been turned off.

With the arrangements made, we left, with six days to wait until the day of our marriage. I found it difficult to sleep the night before; I didn't believe we could just sneak into the registry office to get married and then be allowed to leave unchallenged, considering that so many people now knew of our intentions.

We finally arrived there at the appointed time. I was relinquishing my birth name of Barbara Shaw to become Mrs. Barbara Clements, having given up my maiden name of Barbara Hall to become Mrs. Barbara Worrall in 1945 at the Bristol Registry Office. Confusing? I'll say... and that is just the beginning of the muddle.

This was not to be the end of our marital adventures. Clem put out a smoke screen as, after considerable press and media attention, there had been no arrest at my first attempt at becoming a bigamist. So, we notified the press of our intention to marry yet again on Valentine's Day 1992 ? only nine months after my second marriage of 1991. In the November we travelled once again to Nottingham Registry Office and purchased another birth certificate for Barbara Shaw. This was Clem's trump card; he knew officialdom would believe that Barbara Shaw was attempting to use that name to obtain another marriage, but this was not the case. He had anticipated every move, his strategy was marvellous. He persuaded me to distance myself from the names of Hall and Shaw by swearing a change of name deed at a solicitor's office – a simple enough procedure at a minimal cost. I was now to be known by the name of Barbara Goss, Goss being the maiden name of my biological mother mentioned on the birth certificate of Barbara Shaw. Nothing wrong there, it would have been the only legal name that I could have been entitled to.

So now I had given up my name of Barbara Shaw and adopted the name of Barbara Goss but, for a second successful bigamous marriage, we had to be so precise with the law. During a meeting with solicitors, it transpired that I now had to give up my right to the name of Barbara Hall; I was now officially Barbara Goss. It was a good thing that Clem knew what he was doing, because I sure didn't at the time (have I mentioned that he is a mastermind?)

I have no doubts about my love and devotion for this man; he has never for one minute thought of throwing in the towel. Battle on is Clem's war cry in the face of adversity; never relent or give in. Freedom of speech is your inherent right, use it to your advantage, make the freedom bestowed upon us yours and then share it with others.

A few days before our planned Valentine's Day marriage we had selected the witnesses who would be required to attend, and set off to the chosen venue. This was not to be in

Birmingham as would be expected because of our domicile, but Clem didn't tell me where we were going, it was to be another surprise outing.

Our journey ended at West Bridgford Hall, the council building where marriages were conducted and where we again went through the formalities required by the Registrar who, incidentally, informed Clem that he was illegitimate. We presented the vital document – my change of name deed, and it was accepted as proof of the person wishing to marry, namely Barbara Goss formerly Barbara Hall. Everything went according to plan and with the special licence we left, intending to return for our marriage on St. Valentine's Day.

The day arrived for my third marriage, and I should have been quite used to it by now, but no, the sheer anticipation of it caused me to be anxious. I was very, very uneasy and wanted to call it off. However, I did go through with it and became Clem's wife for the second time. As there had been no divorce from my former husband, technically my two marriages to Clem were illegal, but on the other hand, I had also been led to believe that because of the false information on my birth certificate, my first marriage was not legally recognised.

I could not capture my moment of jubilation, because the camera turned out to be faulty. But still, I was married and that mattered more than anything to me, although we were positive that arrests would follow and Clem was most determined, otherwise our daring ventures would have been a waste of time and money.

However, because I had no official identity, I could not be charged with any offence, so we could not plead our case in court and I did not therefore get the breakthrough I had hoped for which may have helped in getting the question of my true identity resolved. The situation remained unchanged for the time being at least. The Press had notified the general public of our intention to marry on Valentine's Day, some three months prior to the day. A further birth certificate had been applied for on 19th November 1991 for Barbara Shaw, and the day rapidly approached for our wedding day. We were still living in Handsworth, Birmingham at the time of this second bigamous marriage in order to create confusion as to where it was to take place. This served our purpose admirably; don't keep all your eggs in one basket, as the saying goes. So having provided the details for our forthcoming marriage to the Registrar at the Registry Office at West Bridgford, Nottingham, all was set to go ahead. The details were, to the best of our knowledge and belief, as required by law, and at the time it was the only available information that we could obtain. The stage was set, all we had to do was be there on the day and see what happened, and face the consequences if we were doing wrong.

When we arrived at the Registry office our witnesses were already there. We had chosen a late afternoon wedding as we'd had to travel from Birmingham. Everything was going according to plan, and there was no hitch until the signing of the register, when the Registrar looked at the address we had proffered, and then burst out, "But you are my neighbours!"

Clem, as spontaneous as ever, quickly replied that we were still in the throes of decorating and hadn't moved in yet. The Registrar seemed satisfied, making the comment, "Ah… that would explain why I haven't seen you."

That's how I became married to Clem for the second time in the space of nine months. There have been other attempts for us to marry, we have also been through ceremony of blessings in churches to our iniquitous situation, anything to bring attention to my plight but! All our efforts have been in vane we are still not recognised as husband and wife, which is our dearest wish and what we rightly deserve, one day maybe.

Chapter 41   Vanished Without Trace

Barbara Shaw has disappeared. Barbara Hall never officially existed. She was really Barbara Shaw according to her alleged birth certificate but as Robert Shaw (entered on birth certificate as 'father') never existed, this is a travesty. Barbara Hall became Barbara Worrall when she married George Worrall in 1945. However, because the marriage was not legally recognised, she was told she had no entitlement to the name of Worrall.

Since many firms of solicitors considered the marriage to be illegal, Barbara Worrall reverted back to spinsterhood and changed her name to that of her so-called mother Violet and her Aunt Lily's maiden name of Goss.

Having become a spinster again, and adopting her rightful (illegitimate) name of Barbara Goss, she then married her common law husband Cyril Clements for the second time and, from then on, had two husbands alive and three marriage certificates to show for her audacity.

I sometimes describe myself in the third person, as if I am referring to somebody else, because that is how it feels, as if I really do not exist and never have. There is no genuine record of my birth; my first marriage is not recognised, but then when I attempt to marry Clem, it is suddenly convenient to the authorities to point out that I am already married. So am I married to one husband? Or two Or none?

Both of these marriages were declared null and void, but not through due process of law. We felt so cheated at not having secured for ourselves the possibility of a court hearing to face the consequences of two bigamous marriages. This would have given us the opportunity we needed to get this whole issue sorted out once and for all, but that was not going to be allowed to happen. So, having been denied our day in court, we had to plan our next move.

Then we hit on the idea that if we could be allowed a ceremony of blessing, this would again draw the attention of the press. We went ahead with that and the television cameras were there to record it, but although we were told it went out on TV-am, we have never been able to substantiate whether or not they broadcast the event. It is almost fourteen years since that blessing and now, with the introduction of civil partnership status for all, there may be another chance of establishing the true position regarding my marital status. For myself, I have always wanted these two bigamous marriages publicised extensively; not because I crave the attention, I do not, but it would prove to the world what a hypocritical and damaging society we live in, as well as highlighting the ridiculous situation that I find myself in.

So instead of becoming Barbara Clements as I had hoped, with two marriage certificates for my efforts, I was still as far away from a legal marriage as ever. I remained the woman who never was, without a name to call my own. Unable to say: well it has been a hard struggle, but I know who I am now and can at last move on. No. Alas, I am still Mrs. Nobody and she is not real either. None of it seems to be real. It is said that truth is stranger than fiction. The kind of thing that you read about in novels and mysteries of suspense was happening to me and it was all just so unbelievable.

After a great deal of thought, I finally decided to change my name again by Deed Poll. I was advised and assisted by a top firm of solicitors. They firstly appointed Clem as my Enduring Power of Attorney to protect me from officious bullying, and then my name was officially and legally changed to Jane Doe. We had discovered and been in touch with the legendary Mormons, who provided us with evidence that Violet Goss had married a Sydney Shaw on 18th July 1919, in the Registration District of Nottingham. I could have used any surname, Smith or Bloggs, it made no difference, but we decided on the American pseudonym which identifies a dead person, as in John or Jane Doe, and this is how I am officially known today. However, although I possess a legal document with my chosen name on it, that does not prove who I am, or give me an identity. I still do not know who my true birth parents were, and trying to obtain a passport has been something of a nightmare because I could not satisfactorily answer the questions which related to my birth.

I know that with the help of a legal team I have been brought through the system with parallel identities, making it clear to me that when I am requested to give information to a public body, it has to be the truth, the whole truth, and nothing but the truth. It says nothing for my adversaries that their information is based on what records they hold, irrespective of their origins, and no matter how many and whether or not they are true records, which I am certain they are not. But then, they are not on trial; I am. These anomalies are despicable and if we are all to act according to the written law, then I would suggest that should not just include the official bodies, but begin with them.

The fact that I took that journey down memory lane and discovered the cottage some sixty-nine years later, and also received a genuine letter from a person who was told by his mother about the child who was taken away from that cottage by travelling folk, is surely evidence enough that there was foul play involved. It is not rocket science. So how does the argument presented by senior officials who have looked into my case stand up? And surely, after they had offered to take my case to the highest realms, it is not unreasonable of me to ask what they are doing with the vast resources available for such cases as mine, with all their complexities?

If I could dare to make a suggestion to those with all the answers, would it not be beneficial to all concerned to look once again at Public Records – in particular the record of the birth of one Barbara Shaw? Then, with the assistance of an experienced legal team, make a detailed and thorough search for the birth record of Barbara Hall? If this is not permissible in law, then I am most certainly vanished without trace. Should I now accept, with the issue of my passport, that I have been reborn from the date of issue and now have to concede that I have been searching for the Woman Who Never Was?

My wish (maybe only a dream) is for this to take place before it becomes recognised as the scandal of the century. When I consider that I have two husbands alive to the present day and, at the last count, I have twenty-nine grandchildren, thirty-three great-grandchildren and an unknown number of great-great-grandchildren, I begin to question my sanity. How and why did this all come about? Was I responsible in some way because I refused to accept what I have always believed to be a mockery – a tissue of lies concocted to keep me quiet? What woman in her right mind would take all this lying down?

Until the official body presents me with some tangible proof that Barbara Shaw and Barbara Hall are one and the same person, my pursuit of the truth continues; I will never capitulate. Until then, my requests for a review of my pension claim will never be taken seriously. Each attempt falls down at the first hurdle – the establishment (or not) of my true identity. But I have never yet been given an official decision in writing and therefore have always been denied the chance to appeal against any such decision.

There is much discussion these days about human rights; in the light of my own experiences, I feel someone, somewhere is deliberately missing the point. If I could successfully claim my pension rights, backdated to the time of my legal entitlement, I could fulfill my dream of taking a luxury cruise around the Mediterranean. If the reader thinks this is wishful thinking, then I would agree with them entirely, for I have never had anything of any value to look forward to in my entire life.

Clem, my rightful husband, has of course been my rock; a constant support to me and a joy to be with, always. I owe him a debt of gratitude that I will never be able to repay and, of course, he asks for nothing in return. But my one great comfort is in just knowing that he feels the same sentiments as I do and, that alone is sufficient to outweigh the sorrow and cruel memories of my past.

It is my intention to embark on something that can only be beneficial to me. It is something that has been planned for a very long time and, when it finally happens, it should create unprecedented sales of my book in today's markets. Any proceeds from the sales will be applied to secure the best legal brains in the country to discover why officers of Nottingham City Council believed they had a God-given right to prevent me from discovering my biological parentage.

The documents I hold were issued with the knowledge of the issuer by virtue of the warning: CAUTION – Any person who (1) falsifies any of the particulars on this certificate, or (2) uses a falsified certificate as true, knowing it to be false, is liable to prosecution. It was in 1968 that Clem notified the Registrar at Shakespeare Street, Nottingham, that the information on my supposed birth certificate was false. He encountered belligerence and disdain and was warned off in no uncertain terms: 'This has nothing to do with you, you are not her husband; mind your own business.' Clem just politely bade them good-day and walked away, saying to me, "Don't worry; I will be back to fight another day." This is what I admired in Clem – a true fighter in every sense of the word. His attitude to my inconceivable problem has never diminished, he is still as resolute as ever that one day we will have the answers, and it is their turn to capitulate.

Chapter 42   I, Barbara...

My wedding day, you will recall, had its awkward moments, but in spite of these, my marriage to George Worrall went ahead and I felt it was a day of personal triumph for me. After living for nearly seventeen years with Robert and Violet Hall for parents and, Lily the spiteful half-sister, the day I became a wife meant that, although now one half of a new partnership, I was free from their influence. Free to be myself, to express myself without being the target of their vulgar and derisory remarks. I just took it for granted that my life would take a similar course to that of other young married couples whom I knew; that we would settle down in our own little abode and raise a family and, to quote the old fairytales, 'live happily, ever after'.

I had naturally given no thought to any problems which might crop up because of issues about my birth certificate and it was only later – twenty-two years later, in fact – that I began to have misgivings about my birth and parentage and began making enquiries. The second issue of my supposed birth certificate was dated 18th, July 1967. I believe it was this birth certificate and not the one issued some three years earlier that sent me off the rails, because now I had come to realise how false my life had been. I had not yet met up again with Clem at this time, contrary to what certain people believed and suggested, '...oh, come on Barbara, you don't expect us to believe that; surely it wasn't just a chance meeting, that sort of thing only happens in novels; pure fiction...'etc, etc. At one time all that talk used to affect me, but now after all these years it doesn't bother me at all. Some of those who made the remarks have since hit stormy waters. I feel no satisfaction from their downfalls, but they should not judge others by their own standards. However, I do remember every last one of them.

At the time my first-born came along, I was living at the Balaclava Pub on Denman Street, Radford, Nottingham. It was not a public house during the time I was there, a couple called Jack and Winnie Widdowson rented the property. They had one son who had been born there, and my half-sister and her husband also lived there with their four children. Jack would chop sticks for a living and then sell them on to the local shops. We often helped in his firewood business, which was carried out in the cellar of the property.

George, my husband, joined us after he was demobbed from the navy. I believed then that I was on the threshold of a new life; to me it meant everything that a young woman could want, but it seemed that there was always some trouble lurking around the corner. My life didn't get off to the start I had hoped it would. I had Shirley, my newborn daughter, to consider, and it was obvious that the bed-sitting room we rented was totally inadequate and unsuitable; certainly not the place in which to start married life. We had a fire and a bed, and it was a start, but we had planned to have more children.

George returned to his profession of French polishing, and went on to become solely in charge, he trained many young women in the art. Whilst I was living at the Balaclava pub I conceived my second child (George junior), so we had to make a move before his birth was due. On 19th February 1938, my half-sister Lily Shaw married Gerald Oldham when they were living at 589 Carlton Road, Carlton, Nottingham. Her second daughter, Sheila, was born at 7 Denman Street, Nottingham, which was the postal address for the Balaclava pub where we were all living. Previous to that, Lily had registered her first-born, Christine Ann in her adopted name of Lily Hall, and the address on the birth certificate was 66 Blue Bell Hill Road, Nottingham. Years later she claimed she never lived there and, as we are not permitted to enquire why, this appears to be yet another wrongful registration.

Clem was given permission to obtain copies of these documents in 1990, to help him to put some semblance of a family tree together. What he discovered, to his horror, was that the registration system had created more problems than it should have solved. A miracle was what was needed, but he knew that wasn't going to happen, and he didn't want to go around asking awkward questions, and upsetting the family over his findings. He believed discretion to be the better part of valour and decided to do a bit of sleuthing before he approached what had become a delicate subject.

Whilst he was researching my past, I could see that he was becoming irritable; there were endless questions but no answers, nothing was making any sense at all. He called it a magnificent deception, no wonder he was concerned by it all.

"You have been had," he would say, "well and truly stitched and mailed. But still, I am not ready to give up, I'll train myself to look for what I am supposed to see and then maybe it could give me a clue as to what has been recorded which appears to be wrong."

He said that all we needed was a foothold, and then if we could explain our findings, more information might be forthcoming. We had already established that Robert Mark Shaw never existed and it could well have been Robert Mark Hall who applied that name because I was his daughter and he wasn't married to my mother. That was the simplest explanation but without his confirmation, it was worthless. Maybe he was afraid of prosecution, which was inevitable had he been found out, but again this was not an avenue to explore and also didn't explain why I was abandoned until I was nearly five years of age. What we had to decide was whether Robert Mark Hall and Sydney Shaw was one and the same person. We had confirmation that Robert Mark Hall was born on 10th November 1901 at Grove Road, Halton, Whitkirk, near Leeds; his father was Mark Hall and his mother was Elizabeth Hall, formerly Burnell. These families could have originated out of Ireland in 1827 and 1831 respectively, the latter having been incarcerated in the workhouse at the age of sixteen.

By the time I married, the seed of secrecy had already been sown, and I am frequently asked this question: if I had known at the time of my marriage to George Worrall that my official name was Barbara Shaw, would I have still married? Silly question. I was in love, so for sure I would, my answer would have to be yes, but had I known the truth about my birth certificate then, I would not have the identity crisis I have today. I would still be looking for my biological father; it's just that the questions would be different. It is still a deception, no matter from which angle you look, and I have unknowingly inherited a legacy of lies that have continued unchecked and unsolved.

The deeper we dig into family background, the more embedded we become, and the more challenging it all becomes, so who are my immediate family and what was my purpose to be? Where was I to fit into a family environment befitting of my birthright? Oh dear! I didn't see this coming I don't have any. What a nightmare. My search to find the answers continues, and I wholeheartedly admit that it is getting me down. Surely I am due something such as an admission of guilt from somebody? I now know my immediate family, but only by association and not by relation. I was told I was illegitimate and would remain so for the rest of my natural life, with no documentary evidence to prove otherwise.

Don't weaken, they say, there will be a silver lining. It seems more like a lead lining to me… impenetrable, certainly. If only Lily would have opened up more, things could possibly have been resolved long ago. So she is my half-sister by my so-called mother and different father, but that doesn't make her a natural relation, and if I am illegitimate I have no natural relatives, only those I create through marriage.

There is no way that I can think of that which would help me alleviate my present situation other than claiming the right under the Freedom Of Information Act 2004 to see the details of my birth, not those provided by the midwife Sarah Ellen Wheatley but! Those of the Medical Officer of Health, which would have been notified by him to the Superintendent Registrar where the inception of birth would take place.

I was always told I was a bastard. Violet in particular delighted in telling me so at every opportunity. A decision I took in 1995 was to distance myself from these weird family names and start afresh with a brand new name that would close the door on any further tampering and speculation. So, when, on 23rd March 1995, I, Barbara... became Jane Doe by deed poll, it turned out to be a happy chapter in my life. I now know who I am, for the first time ever. What I don't know is who I was before. So you see I just cannot give up the struggle until I have the last vestige of what went so terribly wrong and why? I am still seeking answers and will continue to do so, irrespective of the consequences.

Chapter 43   Happy Ending Or Will It Be?

It is inconceivable that somebody can come through eighty-four years of their life without knowing who they are; worse still, that somebody is me.

I now know that I am Jane Doe. My passport says so. Other than that, it reveals nothing of my past... difficult to imagine but that's how my life has been for as long as I can remember. Even though I have moved on from my inexplicable beginnings and, with Clem's help, have carved out a new life for myself, I am still troubled by the uncertainty of my future.

Our Ruby anniversary will soon be here, when Clem and I will have been together as man and wife for forty years, even though we still cannot claim that right legally. Hopefully, on the day of our anniversary, 16th October, it could all change dramatically when we enter the church of Saint Mary and Saint Nicholas in Beaumaris, Anglesey, North Wales.

I went missing at the age of four; eighty years later, I am lost forever. All hope of discovering who I am is a lost cause; I am not permitted to know as I have been a subject under the Official Secrets Act since I discovered that the maiden name I held and grew up with, believing it to be my rightful title, was nothing but a figment of someone's imagination. I had to wait until I was forty-one years of age to learn of this travesty in my life, and I am sure any feeling person would understand what an indescribably cruel blow it was to me, especially as I had unknowingly married under a false identity and raised a family of six.

My life has passed me by, but surely this was an intentional and deliberate act by those who register and hold such records and then have the power to conceal them from prying eyes until the year 2038, and even to put these records beyond subpoena. I have no precise plans for the future... who could predict with any certainty when their life holds so much uncertainty? I have very definite ideas of what I would like to be able to do, but whatever happens, I shall still strive to secure the truth to my whole sorry episode, alongside and, with the unfailing efforts of Clem who has been there throughout, for almost forty-one years.

I am now beginning to realise why Clem chose the name Jane Doe for me. It was a master stroke on his part and, as he says, my case has to impress if it is to serve justice not only for me but for others in a likewise situation. The tenacity of this man, my husband, never ceases to amaze me; he never gives his brain a rest, always so active in mind and body, giving his all and getting pleasure from whatever he becomes involved in. I have no words to describe what I truly feel for him; he is just the most amazing person and if anyone can solve this riddle, he can.

There has not been a time that I can recall when those I have sought answers from have ever answered me truthfully. I am not accusing them of lying to me, but of only giving me half the truth and being very evasive about the most important aspects of my life. For all the use that is to me, I would prefer them either to remain silent or to lie about everything and have done with it, then at least they would be pure lies and that would give me somewhere to begin... how can you begin when half the lies are true?

One day the truth will out; maybe this will be too late for me, but of some consolation is that family members could, if they so wished, delve into the mystery of my past. It is an intriguing story – so far without an ending; probably there is no ending and until the truth is established, I will keep wandering, just as I did with the travelling people all those years ago.

When I first became aware that I was not whom I was supposed to be, it was a hammer blow that I could not adjust to, something that, at the time, tore into my heart and I was unable

to share that pain with a living soul. It was a secret not to be
shared until I knew more. My so called parents were the ones to
ask, but I had no idea where they were; I had not seen them in
years and didn't care to, if I am honest. I had never been treated
by them as a daughter should have been and the memory of the
abuse lives on in my mind from the very first day it all began. I
will never, ever forget... it was so cruel, and someone knows
more than they're letting on. How could anyone live with that
knowledge? Have they no consciences?

       To my mind, if I were to discover who I really was, it
could have detrimental consequences for somebody, even to the
present day. Mystifying it may be, but how am I to explain the
enigma that is my life without pointing the finger of suspicion in
whatever direction I am led. Isn't it a free country? Yes,
apparently, for all except me. I have been burdened with the
onus of proving who I really am – a daunting task when much of
the documentation I hold, supposedly relating to me, is
erroneous from its inception and leads me down one dead end
after another. I can tell you, it is beginning to irritate me.

       If I am that child born on 20th May, 1923 – the very day
that the Prime Minister resigned from office – and was registered
on 9th June, 1923 at the Registry Office in Shakespeare Street,
Nottingham as Barbara Shaw, how come I vanished without
trace for forty-one years to re-emerge under a different name
with no one prepared to answer my questions of how it could
have happened and why?

       It is vital that I seek out these answers, to enable myself
to challenge the courts as to what went so dramatically wrong
with my life. Another burning question is why have the many
solicitors, engaged and paid through the legal aid system, not
resolved a single problem or found a resolve to my ludicrous
situation? I can only conclude that these individuals are
charlatans of the worst order, who took on my case for personal

gain, not caring a jot that their bungling interference only exacerbated and prolonged the mental anguish I had inherited because of a tissue of lies.

Deprivation and alienation has been the order of the day ever since I tried to run away from my past. I know now that my past will never leave me. I wake up with this trauma, I go to sleep with it, my dreams turn into nightmares and somehow I feel the guilt of it all, as if it is I who should stand accountable for creating such a fuss over nothing. But to me it is everything; is it so wrong to want a happy ending? In these politically correct times, with the Freedom of Information Act and the constant calls for more transparency, am I asking too much? I don't think so.

If someone were to ask me who I felt had most let me down throughout my quest and who would I blame, I would have to reply, most decidedly, the entire legal establishment for their utter incompetence. My case would not have dragged on for so long if they had set out to accomplish some satisfactory resolve amicable to both sides. I, after all, am the innocent party in all of this; I cannot be held responsible and brought to account for matters I was too young to have any control over.

For me it would be truly remarkable to say I now know who I am, or should have been; that I could now right the wrongs and fight the good fight for my pension rights (all nineteen years that I am owed), leave these shores for a warmer climate. In my dreams… do you think I would be allowed to spread my story across the seven seas? Very unlikely. I am nearing the end of my nightmare journey – entirely of my own volition. I would not be compelled by anyone to give up the right to know who dumped this dilemma at my door but, because of exhaustion, I must take a break for awhile. Then I can return with renewed vigour and maybe a different strategy to solve this age old mystery. My worrying days are over; I don't believe that any more can be achieved at this late stage. Life has passed me by all these years, and I shall have to live with that come what may. Changing my life now makes no matter because, in my heart of hearts, I know that I could not play the cards that were dealt me any differently. I must try now to put most of it behind me, and devote more time to Clem; to try to help him enjoy his retirement which is long overdue. I do believe that I could identify my biological father or point the finger of suspicion, but then I would probably be accused of libel. However, you cannot libel the dead and as I am almost eighty-five years of age my father, whoever he was, is surely dead, God rest his soul.

I promise you this: when I bounce back from my nightmare journey and reveal everything I know, it will provoke much discussion. I know it will all be glossed over by declaring me a crank. Well, I don't give a damn – I can live with that. Does anyone imagine this hasn't been declared already? I am constantly ignored in my endeavours, even after two bigamous marriages, and still it all remains the big secret. I say come out into the open and reveal the facts and behave humanely. All I want is to have my case heard, to bring about a full disclosure of the facts, but though I am desperate, I will not kneel down and beg for the truth... why should I?

Those who are new to my story may wonder, quite rightly, from which planet I came. True, I am an alien, but not in that context. I was made aware of this when one of my many grandchildren, hugged me and then declared, 'Grandma, I have tried to do a family tree and it stops with you; I cannot trace anything back from your marriage, it is almost as if you had landed from space.' This unsettled me in a way I find hard to describe. I was also unnerved by it, and I am sure she was aware how taken aback I was. After giving it a lot of thought, I realised she was absolutely correct. We lost touch with her for a number of years until her renewed contact with us a few weeks ago, when an e-mailed greeting card brought tears of joy into my eyes. In her e-mails; she disclosed that Clem and I, Darran our son, my son George (her father) and his wife were the only living family on her side. Without authentic documents, how will she or anyone else prove their line of descendancy with my false birth certificate and faulty marriage? I am told that to receive certain benefits such as state pension and housing benefit, I would have to satisfy various departments that Barbara Shaw and Barbara Hall was one and the same person. All can I say to that is, I was not the author of this magnificent deception, and I will not bow or humble myself to anyone, and be damned.

Chapter 44   Legacy Of Lies

It often seems to me that my life has been one big lie (my birth certificate certainly is!) and I have been consistently lied to and deceived in my battle to uncover the truth. I continue to be driven by a burning desire to get to the bottom of this mystery; to discover not only what were the circumstances of my birth, but also why they were concealed at the time and, even more disturbing, have been the subject of a cover-up ever since.

It was not until I moved in to live with Clem that I realised my whole life had been one long conspiracy. From the very moment I walked out on my family in the autumn of 1967, there was a new meaning and purpose to my every thought. Everything seemed strange, and yet much clearer than at any time that I had spent in my marriage and bringing up a family. It is difficult to put into words, but there was a noticeable change that I could detect for myself. I had come alive all of a sudden, and this was a different life, so vibrant I felt that I could now make plans for the future.

I have asked myself repeatedly, was it selfish to want something in my life for the first time ever, and was it wrong of me to want to confide in someone who was prepared to listen to the problems of my daunting past? I gave no thought to what I was doing any more; my decisions were hasty, I knew I was in love, and it seemed right at the time. All my life I had been starved of love, and now I had it in abundance. Surely this is what turned my head and invited me to look in another direction? If that was so wrong, then one day I shall be judged. Then I go into another vein of thinking: wasn't I let down so badly throughout my entire life by everyone whom I put my trust in? Did I not deserve some recompense for becoming a chattel over the years, having no one to talk to about my doubts and fears? Didn't I deserve better for the efforts I had made to ensure that everything was just the way it should be with a devoted wife and mother?

My mind will never cease from looking back into the past for answers which I now know will never come. I can live and accept that my life will remain a best kept secret, and that, because of reasons way beyond my control, the truth will never be revealed until the year 2026. I am fully aware that I will not be around when that day arrives, but some of those who are endeared to me will be. I would like to feel in my heart of hearts that they will visit me wherever I am laid to rest, and just say: sorry, we misjudged you; we got it wrong.

Our accusers now stand accused; further development has come to light through a member of the family that shows they were aware that something was terribly wrong with my life when they heard me talking with a neighbour who lived close by. It appears that I was in conversation and had been discussing my birth certificate, telling her that my real name, according to the birth certificate, was really Barbara Shaw, and what could I do about it? I remember the occasion, but not all of what was said. My daughter would have been only twelve years of age then, and didn't understand or attach much importance to it at the time, but she remembered the conversation better than I did. I have often wondered if she said anything after I left them all. Even though it was such a long time ago, I hope that they may think of me differently now that the facts are out in the open.

On another occasion, an even younger daughter recalled something that also added credence to what I had been stating over many years, about my alleged National Insurance number ZW.07.76.70.D, when she said that it couldn't be mine as she was only ten months old at the time of issue, (24th September 1956) and she knew that I would never have left her to go and seek work some two hundred miles away. If I had done so, it would have been a talking point within the family. It didn't become a talking point because it never happened, and those who say it did are guilty of slander. I repeat... it was not me. I don't know who it was and, that should be an end to the matter even though I know it won't; I am continually being pressed for answers I don't have, but the irony is that I am the one who needs answers!

My legacy of lies is out of control; there are too many... they have never been nipped in the bud. This, for me, is a bitter pill to swallow; why should anyone tell such a blatant lie and escape detection and accountability? I am fully aware that my case history is 'Statute Barred', but surely this does not prevent me from instituting a civil action if and when I have the funds to support such a case? Our day in Court would be a marvellous achievement; I would be deliriously happy – over the moon – with the opportunity to put the record straight once and for all.

The first time I was really aware that lies were being bandied around was shortly after I left my abode where I had been so happy for twenty-two years. It was the discovery of my birth details in 1964 that started my unease and unrest and eventually brought about my departure from the family whom I loved with all my heart. If mine and Clem's paths had not crossed (for the better, I might add), I could still be at home with my family and they would know nothing of what I had endured when I was a young girl. I would have received my pension jointly through my husband's contributions, and no one would have been any the wiser... but! And this is a big BUT!

Was it intended for my past upbringing to be revealed, considering that I discovered purely by accident that someone had tampered with my birth details? In all, as I remember, I visited that Registry Office three times because I believed that they held the birth details of me, Barbara Hall. It was that same office that approved my marriage on 5th May 1945. At that time, I had never seen a birth certificate for myself; Barbara Hall was the name I knew was on my marriage certificate, so you see I was in no doubt about my birth certificate – it would verify that I was the same Barbara Hall… wouldn't it?

Although my life had been quite maligned at times, I was not expecting anything sinister when applying for my birth details. Certainly I was totally unprepared for what I read on the certificate that was eventually handed over to me… informing me that I was not Barbara Hall, but someone else. When I dared to query it and was told on the last occasion to remove myself forthwith from the office or else, my life went into meltdown and stopped dead from that moment. I was constantly asking myself the question: how could it be? How could it have happened… what could I do about it?

Right from the beginning, when I first entered the registry office and gave my name, I sensed that I was an unwelcome visitor, and indeed my first two visits got me nowhere; I was just put off with excuses. I was at a disadvantage because I had no idea what was going on – only that something was terribly wrong. That much I knew and the realization hit me like a ton of bricks when I had sight of that birth certificate for the very first time. 'There is no mistake!' I was told. Awe-struck, I was welded to the spot where I stood; staring at these erroneous details that glared belligerently back at me. It was then that the true feelings of my life flooded back to me; the doubts had always been there, but I'd pushed them away, out of my conscious mind. Now they were surfacing, and I just broke down and sobbed bitterly and uncontrollably. The devastation in my life was here to claim recompense; it was payback time, but for what… and what had I done to deserve it?

I felt so miserable and so alone, but I somehow had to shrug it off; I had my young daughter with me in her pushchair and, I had drawn the attention of passers by. Goodness knows what they thought, and I don't know what I would have said if anyone had ventured to ask me what was wrong. I was so wretched and dejected that I couldn't have put my feelings into words even if I had known how to. I could not stifle the sobbing so I beat a hasty retreat.

From that day, I learned a lot more about aspects of my life which were only memories but suddenly took on more sinister meanings. I have not been provided with the answers I need because my life has been metaphorically rubber-stamped. RESTRICTED, CLASSIFIED, TOP SECRET. This would be fine for some, I daresay; they may even enjoy the 'importance' of being such an enigma, but it doesn't cut with me. I want to know the truth, and I want to know now. It is my right to know and I cannot be prevented from knowing; you in your ivory towers – do your worst, it won't make the slightest difference. I am still here, the same old nuisance, asking the same old questions, continuing in my fight for the facts, willing to do whatever it takes to shake your resolve, and to finally get at the truth.

Chapter 45   Full Disclosure

"As you are well aware, the facts of your circumstances are quite unique. We do not believe we can assist you further." What is that supposed to mean? I do not know to what extent my case has been delved into by this particular firm of solicitors in Caernarfon. Certainly they have never made me aware that they did not have the legal ability to proceed with my case to the doors of the court, as discussed at my initial interview. At that time they seemed confident that they could resolve the identity problem so that I could be properly compensated for the loss of my state pension for all those years when I should have been able to relax and enjoy my retirement. Instead of which, I have suffered unnecessary anxiety over money, and there has been little to enjoy; without Clem, I would have gone under long ago... maybe that was part of the plan.

When I was recently issued with a passport in my chosen name of Jane Doe, I felt it was the beginning of the end of my troubled past and that I could now look forward to a brighter future. I certainly, grossly under-estimated the power of those, who would stop at nothing to prevent the full disclosure of my life, since being kidnapped, at the age of four. The new world I was expecting to encounter still seems to be a million miles away and I am no nearer my goal than when I first posed the question, 'Who am I?'

So this is just another solicitor who has deserted us, of the hundreds we have engaged over the years to solve the mystery of my birth – why I was registered as Barbara Shaw but compelled to live most of my life as Barbara Hall? If there had been a paper trail from my birth for either Barbara Shaw or Barbara Hall, I could have lived with that and apportioned the blame to my so-called parents, Robert Mark and Violet Hall/Shaw. But the fact that there is no paper trail at all is very

248

mystifying and suggests a cover up at the time of my birth. Even more intriguing is that the cover up has remained in existence until the present day and is likely to continue.

To the best of my knowledge and belief, Robert Mark Hall was a nobody; with no ambition or calling, and at the time of my abduction was just a gipsy, or traveller, as he preferred to be known. As far as I know, he did nothing useful with his life, but fell foul of the law on occasions when he committed petty crimes.

However, undaunted, I still have another hopeful avenue to explore. I have received a letter from a clergyman whom I met in North Wales. He said it was a pleasure to meet Clem and myself, and he took a personal interest in my lifelong problem of non-identity. In his letter, he confirms that he will be pleased to help with our wedding plans and help to bring about a happy conclusion to our long and difficult journey. We would have to look into the details, of course, but I suppose there is every possibility that Clem and I could marry for the third time (my fourth marriage in total) and this could possibly turn out to be the only legal marriage out of them all.

But what an abominable situation to find oneself in at the age of eighty-four; I would not wish such a predicament on my worst enemy, not that I am aware I have any enemies – only those who constantly block my path to the truth.

Clem, having discovered that his origins are in the Republic of Ireland, and being the holder of an Irish passport, would be perfectly entitled to take me to his country of birth and marry me there. Such a marriage would be legally bound by the laws of the land. This desire to become Clem's lawful wife in Ireland is the perfect solution to my identity problem. I will rightfully be Mrs. Jane Clements-Doe, and will then be in possession of two legal documents of identity. They will prove nothing about my birth, but they will stand up to scrutiny by any legislative body that wishes to challenge them. I cannot wait for that day, and I am ready to do battle, but this time with confidence that I will be the victor for once in my life.

I have stated many times that it is beyond my comprehension and belief that it has taken half my lifetime to establish an identity that will satisfy officialdom. I now have the freedom, if I so desire, to leave the country and take a holiday abroad. However, there are still certain state benefits to which I am entitled but cannot claim, due to the total of nine – yes, nine, National Insurance numbers which are written into my passport, and no fewer than five NHS numbers.

No matter how I have tried, I have been unable to distance myself from these numbers, despite consulting solicitors privately and through the legal aid scheme. My efforts came to nothing and I am forced to accept and use ZW077670D, even though I have supporting evidence that this number was never issued to me. The Department for Work and Pensions, with their customary logic, has stated that no one else is using this number, so in all probability it must be mine. Thanks a million! Are they sure it wasn't a spare, floating around aimlessly, and they thought they would add it to my rapidly growing collection? This number entered the system on 24th September 1956 and I was two hundred miles away on that day! But I have never been allowed the opportunity to prove my case.

A similar situation exists in relation to NHS number RMCU74/4, issued in 1939 to Barbara Hall of 239 St Ann's Well Road, Nottingham. I was not, and never have been, a member of that household, so how could it have been issued to me, even ignoring the fact that Barbara Hall did not officially exist? This number is therefore not mine and is probably one of the reasons why I find it so difficult to get the medical treatment I need. At the moment my vision is very poor due to cataracts in both eyes, but I seem to have been forgotten about – disregarded as usual. I suffered extreme deafness which was very trying for me and those who tried to communicate with me. Eventually, after the customary battles to establish my entitlement, I was fitted with hearing aids and I am grateful, but it all could and should have been so much easier and earlier in my life why did no one understand my predicament?

I realise that one important move would be for me to enter the courts on a Full Disclosure Clause; it would then be left to the realms of the court to arrive at a satisfactory conclusion of what happened, when and why. The reasons should be revealed for my being taken in the first place by this strange couple who claimed to be my parents. I have learned that they were kin, though how close is a mystery; they were dark-skinned, swarthy gypsies and I was a blue-eyed blonde. The question of my biological parentage will be a matter for the court, possibly the Supreme Court Family Division where my change of name deed was registered in 1995. I did receive a letter from the Master of the Rolls who simply said that my chosen name of Jane Doe was unusual. His interest ended there and so it was not possible to offer any explanation or ask for advice. There have been so many times when I have felt thoroughly sick of the whole business but now I think, well at least I am Jane Doe with a sensational story which I want to share with the world. They say truth is stranger than fiction; in my case I could not agree more – and some of it is completely unimaginable in this the twenty-first century – so bizarre you could not make it up!

The day is drawing ever nearer and I am very anxious. Who wouldn't be? a few weeks away from my wedding day with a lot to do to make it my day of all days. I shall be married in church in a simple cream coloured two piece suit with matching shoes and handbag. Having blue eyes I may wear blue earrings and necklace and maybe knot a blue silk scarf loosely at my throat. Clem has decided to wear a grey suit; no decision yet as to what colour shirt and tie, but I believe he will be looking great on our big day, which I never thought would come.

Clem is almost seventy-seven years of age and still as sharp as a razor. People think he is brilliant; I know he is – I certainly would have got nowhere without him and I cannot think of anyone who would want to take on such a challenge. But Clem will tackle the highest mountain with the remark that it's all in a day's work. That is Clem; no one will ever change him. There must be a few others like him, who adopt the motto of the SAS, Who Dares Wins.

My life has never been easy to explain and I have found that those closest to me, who should understand, have been the first to desert me. To them, I have made a fuss about nothing and they have shrugged it off as meaningless. However, I have a forgiving heart – how can they possibly know how it feels to have your whole life stolen from you?

I believe that Clem deserves better for his endeavours on my behalf; he also has given up more than half his lifetime in the pursuit of my true identity. A jubilant celebration? I don't think so – it has been too long coming. We will go, as planned, for a quiet wedding, and if the press wants their stories, all well and good, we will not stop them from reporting the event. Our marriage will certainly be a hot topic if it is allowed to go ahead and, so far, the clergyman in question can see no reason why it shouldn't. Yet I feel sure there will be a snag somewhere – a fly will get into the ointment if it can.

But the fact of the matter is that although both Clem and I are identified by our birth certificates, his father, Philip George Clements, was once a living person, whereas mine, Robert Mark Shaw, never existed. Our quest to establish the truth has so far taken half a lifetime and we are still no nearer to finding out. But I do feel more hopeful; I have laid down plans for the future and if I achieve my ambition I will be the happiest woman alive and I feel this might inspire other family members to make an effort to delve into the past, to discover the truth that has lain hidden for so long and the reasons behind the cover-ups. Already there are signs of awakening among some of the family, more than I ever hoped for, and quite unexpected. I don't feel so isolated from them now and, at last, there is a glimmer of light at the end of the long, dark tunnel.

Chapter 46   A Best Kept Secret

Dear Family,

I started my book with a letter to you all, so I think it is fitting to end it in a similar vein. You will find it difficult to understand why I left you, and the remorse I have felt. It was not just that I left you – it was inevitable that this would happen one day – but more that you were too young to understand the enormity of the horror and disgust that engulfed me when I realized the truth of my situation.

When I walked out, never to return, I knew how much hurt and heartache you would suffer but, believe me, it was nothing to what I have endured for the forty odd years since I discovered I was officially a 'nobody'. Ask yourselves how you would feel to be told that you were not who you thought you were and officially you did not exist. How do you think it felt to be the mother of six children, but not legally wed? Today, nobody gives a damn about that sort of situation, but personal and social values were very different forty years ago and to have six illegitimate children was unthinkable.

My own mother must have been beside herself with worry. Illegitimacy was even more scandalous in the twenties when I was conceived and I believe she did what she thought was right at the time, to spare me the stigma of being pronounced a bastard. Without proof, I shall never know, but I do believe it possible that Lily knew of Violet's marriage in 1919, and her desperate circumstances prompted her to use her sister's marriage details to register my birth. She would have been unaware that Violet was living apart from Sydney Shaw by then and had taken up with Robert Mark Hall.

Bear in mind that Robert stated to me that it was my Aunt Lily who registered my birth and when Violet found out what she had done, she threw a fit – just one of the many that followed – and I was usually on the receiving end.

I do not have to explain or justify myself to you all. I am not guilty of any crime. Indeed, I have been the victim of an unforgivable miscarriage of justice and you will have to look to others if you want to apportion blame. What I will say is that I have had the good fortune to have Clem to advise me. He has patiently and diligently taken the time and, troubles to do whatever he thought necessary in his efforts to provide me with peace of mind. Nothing has been too much trouble for him and I have been blessed to have such a sensitive and caring man to guide me through those difficult times. Without him I would have been alone, without a friend in the world to share my problems with.

Very soon, my dream will come true, when I am pronounced the legal wife of Cyril (Clem) Clements. Yes, I will officially be Mrs. Jane Clements-Doe after a courtship of forty-one years, even though I have already married him on two previous occasions. Moving on from there, I hope we can marry for a fourth time, on foreign soil, maybe even setting a record, considering I have married the same man four times without breaking the law once.

When I discovered, after three attempts to get at the truth, that I was not Barbara Hall (and therefore could not legally be Mrs. Barbara Worrall, having innocently married under a false name) I was shocked and mortified. George Worrall your father was not interested in my plight or my concerns about it and ignored all my attempts to discuss the problem with him. So tell me, please... who else could I turn to in my shame and misery? I believe that fate played its part when I met my one-time best friend's brother, Clem, in the Mecca Bingo Hall on St Ann's Well Road all those years ago in the autumn of 1967. It was some time before I could bring myself to tell him my secret, but when I took him into my confidence, he vowed that he would not rest until he had helped me to find the truth.

Strangely, in these final stages, the woman who never existed has become something of a celebrity in her own right. The media are just as keen to know the truth of my extraordinary life of who I am and my collection of press cuttings and video clips is growing by the hour.

I have tried to recall when my suspicion was first aroused. But actually, I had always had my suspicions, and who wouldn't after the life I was forced to lead as a child on the road and all the hardships that went with it? Maybe it was wrong of me to keep it all to myself and not share the details with you all, but the occasion never arose. I was an orphan in the storm and so, apparently, were my so-called parents. They were taken into the care of the Cottage Homes, being a euphemism for the Workhouse, where they suffered cruel indignities. After their mother died at an early age, their father couldn't cope and so, in the early nineteen hundreds, that was where they finished up.

I was thirteen when I last saw my Aunt Lily. I adored her. She said to me, "Barbara, you will weep many a bitter tear before you grow much older, but always remember you have..." and because of circumstances beyond my control, I dare not say more for fear of recriminations. I was not sure what she was referring to at the time, but it has all made perfect sense to me since. If only I could provide proof.

So, you see, there was much more to my life than you could ever imagine. It has been shrouded in so much secrecy that most people would not have a clue where to start their search for the missing links. We now have more knowledge of what happened and why, but there are still a lot of things that don't add up. Therefore, our endeavour continues relentlessly until we have the last vestige of truth which will finally lay the ghosts and let us get on with our lives in peace. That is all I have ever wanted – to be at peace.

The answers are still out there and someone knows more about the secrets surrounding my birth than they are prepared to admit. Have no fear; one by one they will be challenged. We are on the threshold of new discoveries since my lawyers have confirmed my present status in life. Even the criminals in society have their rights. Mine have so many times been denied me but rest assured, I will claim my rights, come hell or high water.

I have been described as an enigma that is ironic, because my life has been a puzzle to me from the day I was bundled into the "Varda" to embark upon a life of misery at the hands of the couple who claimed me, but did not want me. But believe me when I tell you that I *will solve this conundrum, even if it takes me to my dying breath. Over the years I was warned never to breathe a word about being kidnapped as a small child and then forced to live as a Romany (with my blonde hair and blue eyes) travelling the highways and byways of a forgotten world. I would not wish my past on another human being and my heart goes out to those who are suffering similar hardships.*

It was a way of life that I was always too ashamed to speak about. It increases your sensitivity and isolates you from the normal way of living until you become such an introvert, you dare not seek friendships. If I had been given a prison sentence for some wrongdoing, I would have served my time and been released. But this has been worse than any custodial sentence; I have been locked away with my secrets for all those years and it has definitely taken its toll, but I am not going to give up the fight until the battle is won.

With my chosen name of Jane Doe and a passport to verify that I am that person, I have been assured by a lawyer that my identity is now accepted and can be used for a marriage in any country of the world. It was interesting that not long ago; the Home Office had also suggested that my birth certificate may be false. After engaging the services of over a hundred solicitors, we were getting nowhere. This, of course, was on the Legal Aid scheme. We did get results when we paid privately, though after shelling out £2,000, it was to learn that my official wartime identity number RMCU74/4 in fact related to one Nellie Orme. Her number has been used as my NHS number and as far as I am aware is still with me today. Nellie Orme, I am sorry, but I played no active part in your identity theft. It was down to the powers that be.

So are you still wondering why I am in a confused state of mind, when all my protestations fall on deaf ears and my arguments are disregarded? The conspiracy theory has always been lurking at the back of my mind, but now it seems clearer to me than ever before. At various times, during interviews, the press have told me, "Oh yes, our readers love a good conspiracy." Perhaps they do. But it has not been enjoyable from where I have been standing... for far too long now.

So if you read this book and my sometimes harrowing account of life as an unknown, and share it with a wider audience, you will not only be doing me a service, but also others who are suffering similar distressing circumstances. It is a pity there are not more people around like Clem, who has been my rock, always at my side, counseling me so that I have been able to come to terms with my legacy of lies. I dare not think about what my life would have been if I had not met him by chance in that bingo hall. I am truly indebted to him, I love him dearly, and I cannot wait for the moment when I will at last be his legal wife.

Finally, it has been overlooked that I was an illegitimate child and have carried that status all of my life. It will go with me when I am lowered into my grave, and on that day, the problem will be yours. What name will you give me when I am laid to rest in hallowed ground? The matter has to be discussed now to avoid legal wrangling and unpleasant arguments.

The name Hall is out of the question and therefore Worrall has to be discounted also. It will be strange, will it not, to be gazed upon with incredulity? I will be more famous in death than I was in life with my Home Office approved name of Jane Doe. I beg you to seek out the truth about my birthright name. Only then can you give me a branch in the family tree and lift this cloud of doubt that still hangs over me. I don't want it to hang over your lives as well.

Dear Family, there I rest my case.

Jane Doe.

EPILOGUE

At long last, my wedding day was upon me. It had been a long wait from my previous planned wedding of Friday 20th May 2011. Having previously paid the sum of £92 to have our vows solemnized on that day my 88th birthday, Clem was anxious that he may have been breaking the law and my marriage would have been considered to be repetitive. After all we had been through a ceremony of marriage on Monday 20th May 1991. The notification of this marriage had been included in the listings for 15 days prior to the scheduled day. Clem was researching his status in this country. He wanted to know his social and professional standing, especially as he had recently been informed he was a stateless person. This worried Clem immensely, because he knew there was much truth in the information provided. He worried about who would look after and care for me, as he had done so, over many, many years, if he were deported. This placed extra burdens on myself. All I dreamed of was to become his legal wife, for ever and a day.

When I awoke on that fateful day (the day that should have been the proudest day of my life, when I had achieved the impossible, to be a legally married woman to the man I love to bits at the over ripe age of eighty-eight), I had a foreboding that this would turn out to be a sinister horrible day. In my mind's eye I just knew it was not to be; I was reduced to bitter tears when I heard Clem say he would not agree to the registrar's terms of deferring the wedding date until he produced his decree of absolution. He knew full well that the registrar was bang out of order and told her so. Does my man know the law? Indeed he does! I couldn't have been more proud of him at any moment than I was then. His stature at that time had grown in inches; there was no stoop about him. I immediately knew he had the foreboding I had; he had just been waiting for the opportunity for the words to be read, which he had chosen: "I declare that I know of no legal reason why I Cyril Clements may not be joined in marriage to Jane Doe", he would have replied emphatically "No!". He has a skilled mind in law. This is why Clem never fails to astound me. Caving in to oppression and tyranny is not in his vocabulary; he is courageous in the face of adversity, a truly remarkable man. I will be proud to be his legal wife one day. I am confident that he and only he will make it happen on his terms and no one else's. His words to the registrar are still ringing wondrously in my ears: "you have cancelled the contract to marry us; we will not negotiate any further; you do not have my consent, therefore without my consent, I request a full refund of monies paid to you."

To say I was bewildered is an understatement. I could think of nothing that could stand in the way. The registry office were well aware of who we were. All the mistakes in my life were public knowledge. The documents of my life were held by them. Surely they, as well as myself, would wish a speedy resolution to the mess they have created with my life. I would like to believe that these mistakes were born out of mal-administration, alas! I now suspect it has been a conspiracy and I am their victim. One day soon I will prove this to be a fact. I know Clem is ready to launch a judicial review against the Registrar for issuing so many flawed documents. A Judicial Revue would take endless years to bring about. There are alternatives to court action, which would cost the earth, especially when an income that we have wouldn't even get us an entrance fee into the solicitors' office. Clem, the strategist that he is, always, always has a contingency plan; he went to bed on Saturday night un-perturbed about the day's events. Unbeknown to me, he was waiting for the opportunity to show how farcical it all was for the likes of me, a Jane Doe, to be legally married. Jane Doe is a non person, much like the John Doe in America, the man with no name, a dead body un-identified. The reason Clem decided on that name for me was because that is an identity which would be very hard to steal. Also he had been contacted by the legendry Mormons regarding me a kidnap victim.

He is unshakeable, resolute as ever, always in control in every crisis and, revered in society and professional circles, he has the ability to pass the time of day on innumerable subjects. I have been witnessed the envious solicitors proclaim that they wish they had his brain. I should be so proud of him, when on occasions there are those who deliberately entice him in a belligerent way, especially the government departments, Department of Work and Pensions, who have recently been informed that Clem is a citizen of the Republic of Ireland. Even though his parents were English, they had been married in Ireland at the Parish Church of Glasnevin, Drumcondra, Dublin Eire on the 6th June 1924. He was christened in the same church in 1931. So our disastrous day on Saturday 3rd September 2011, the day we had chosen to pull off our third marriage to each other, serendipity, we returned to the registry office situated in the Council House, Nottingham on Monday the 5th September 2011, previously they were situated in Shakespeare Street, Nottingham. Where all my problems manifested was at the Shakespeare Registry Office, way back in 1964 that I caught sight of my birth certificate for the first time ever. This was many years before Clem and I met, when I realized it was not in my maiden name of Barbara Hall. My life went into freefall, from which I have never recovered. Most of the jigsaw pieces to my life we have to hand, especially the recently purchased birth certificate for Barbara Shaw, acquired on the 5th September 2011 two-days after the registrar prevented our marriage proceeding at the scheduled time.

The date and time of our marriage was of crucial importance to us. That is why we chose it, it was exactly seventy-two years previously to the chosen time and date, that Neville Chamberlain, in a solemn shaky voice, announced, that the country was at war with Germany. That was on the 3rd September 1939, with the onset of World War 2 I was by then a sixteen year old, making my way through life, having escaped some of the rigours of family life. I was able to stay out of the way of the verbal abuse I had always been a target of. I now had a sense of freedom from the constraints of an abusive household. It was not long before I was issued with a National identity card number RMCU74/4 for Barbara Hall together with a gas mask and a ration book. My war years were spent, mainly with helping the war effort, I worked in the munitions factory based at Colwick in Nottingham. On another occasion I worked at the Royal Ordnance Factory on gun barrels as they came out of the hot ovens; other occasions were packing airman's uniforms in the Nottingham Castle and I put on jodhpurs when I went into the Land Army. All of these vocations were in the name of Barbara Hall. Many times when returning home the sirens would sound; we would all be ushered by the ARP into the nearest shelters as bombs dropped around us, until the all clear was sounded.

I have many vivid memories of these hard times, strange that I, a vibrant Barbara Hall should discover to my horror, that, there is no record of me ever having been born, no record of me working for the Ministry of Defence, or the Agriculture and Fisheries when I was in the Land Army. Mysteriously by the stroke of a pen, I was now Barbara Shaw. These events have played havoc with my life in a devastating way. I have evidence to be able to point my finger of suspicion in the right direction. Many are long gone. For those who remain to torment me in all their guises, I will relentlessly pursue the information I seek. Serendipity has occurred on more than one occasion. I hold the signatures of both of my abductors. If these signatures are authentic, I can now enter the closing stages of why I, an innocent four year old, was taken from a loving caring couple, to wreak upon me this never ending torment and devastation to my life. Should it be now that finally the truth is known, when the authorities in this country open their locked cupboards and record offices to genuine public scrutiny. Then and only then will I be able to put the ghosts of my past behind me. My biological father must have been a man of enormous power. Too unlikely? A fairytale? A Mills and Boon scenario? Perhaps. But until the truth is finally known, it is as feasible a story as any other of the great British cover-up which dogs our closed-shop society. And Barbara Clements, Barbara Shaw, Barbara Hall, Barbara Goss, also known as Jane Doe? Until the truth is established, until I can prove who I am, I am still wandering, as I wandered with the travelling people all those years ago. I am still, despite all my efforts and those of Clem; the "Woman Who Never Was"